HEALTHY FAST FOOD

First published in Great Britain by Simon & Schuster UK Ltd, 2005
A Viacom Company

Simon & Schuster UK Ltd
Africa House
64–78 Kingsway
London
WC2B 6AH

1 3 5 7 9 10 8 6 4 2

Design: **Fiona Andreanelli**
Food photography: **Juliet Piddington**
Home economist: **Kim Morphew**
Stylist for food photography: **Helen Trent**
Copy editor: **Deborah Savage**
Proofreader: **Nicole Foster**

Printed and bound in China

ISBN 0 74325 975 0

Best-kept Secrets of the Women's Institute

HEALTHY FAST FOOD

Liz Herbert

SIMON & SCHUSTER
A VIACOM COMPANY

ACKNOWLEDGEMENTS

I would like to thank my family for their help in many ways during the writing of this book.

To my **'househusband'**, who took over numerous domestic duties after a full day at work himself. And helped, as always, to enhance my limited abilities on the computer.

Also, to the children for their input – particularly in the Whizz Kids chapter – their openness and frankness of opinion, whether spoken or unspoken, which rendered any need for further comment redundant!

CONTENTS

Times change, and with them research updates our knowledge and understanding of how our bodies react to foods – their benefits and drawbacks. Today we rely more than any previous generation on ready-made foods – whole meals previously put together in the factory, ready to be reheated in minutes at home, fast-food chains and sandwich bars, all catering for quick or immediate consumption of food. In a matter of minutes hunger pangs can be satisfied. Their convenience makes them an appealing option, one that provides an instant back up. For those who simply do not have the time (or energy at the end of the day!) to prepare food, 'instant' meals are a lifeline. The important thing is to supplement them with fresh fruit and vegetables, and to not eat them every day.

One of the dangers of mass production on this scale is that it is not immediately obvious just what ingredients go into these meals, and it is up to us, as consumers, to take a closer look at what they contain in order to make informed decisions about what we eat. Only now is research emerging on the possible harmful effects of a diet that depends too heavily on processed food. At the very least it is widely acknowledged that processed foods generally tend to be higher in fat, sugar and salt than home-cooked ones. In addition they are far inferior in taste to home-cooked food and often more expensive. The more processing a food undergoes, the more opportunity there is for nutrients to be lost, be it through discarding some of the substance (say the husk of wheat to make white flour), a cooking process (the heat of which destroys soluble minerals and vitamins), or length of storage time (which affects flavour and nutrient content).

Bad press has been given to E-numbers – claiming they interfere with the ways our bodies work and directly linking them with asthma, eczema, hyperactivity and attention disorders in children – these additives are used by manufacturers to enhance the flavour, colour, shelf life and stability of the food, and are certainly not substances which you would use at home. Many people are sensitive to even minute quantities of chemical residues, colourings and flavourings. Convenience foods are required to detail what they contain, but sometimes the list is so long that it is easy to become bemused half way through!

Children and young people, in particular, are of concern, for their bodies are smaller and more vulnerable to these additives, and unless they learn to cook and eat well they may face a lifetime of living off food that has an accumulating detrimental effect over the years.

The elderly are another vulnerable group: often living on their own and having a small appetite, it requires too much effort to cook just for themselves. They need to be sure that the food that they eat will provide them with the essential nutrients they need.

There are, then, the longer-term implications of the way our eating habits have changed and of a generation brought up with very little knowledge of how to cook. A knowledge and understanding of basic nutrition is the foundation of cooking skills. Armed with only a basic knowledge of nutrition, it will soon become apparent, when you weigh out the ingredients for a recipe, whether the dish will be high or low in calories.

INTRODUCTION

Healthy Fast Food is not a dieting book, in the sense of a weight-loss manual, but hopefully an inspiration to become more aware, and hence take more control, of what you eat, both inside and outside the home. It all comes down to balance – even too much of a relatively nutritious food is harmful in the long term. Good eating habits, a diet with plenty of variety, result in a way of life that is both enjoyable and sustainable. It is not about denying yourself high-calorie foods completely but about being sensible about what you eat, and getting the balance right. For instance, if there is a calorific pudding on offer, go ahead and indulge, but opt for a low-fat main meal with plenty of fresh vegetables to counterbalance the dessert.

The efficient running of our bodies is directly related to the food we eat. So that we look, and feel, well, we need a regular supply of all the different nutrients necessary to enable our bodies to function properly. A healthy diet, combined with regular exercise, is also thought to protect us against disorders such as high blood pressure, some forms of cancer, stroke, heart disease and obesity.

In order to appreciate how to plan your diet, it is necessary to have a basic knowledge of what the main nutrients are, their function in our bodies, and the foods that are rich sources of them.

A QUICK GUIDE TO NUTRITION

Carbohydrates These are divided into sugars and starches, and are mainly a source of energy. Starches (the prime substance of bread, pasta, cereals, potatoes and rice), when unrefined, are known as 'complex' carbohydrates, which means that they release their energy slowly, so that the effects are not apparent so quickly after eating, but will keep us going for longer, say, throughout the whole of the morning. Hence whole-wheat cereals and wholemeal toast are favourites to have at breakfast time. 'Simple' carbohydrates have a lower fibre and vitamin content, because processing strips these out. Sugars provide instant energy, but are pure calories and nothing else.

Proteins Required for the growth and repair of the body's tissues, proteins are found in the greatest quantities in meat, fish, eggs, cheese, nuts, pulses and lentils.

Fats Fats contain about double the calories of carbohydrates, so are twice as fattening! They are divided into two basic categories.

Saturated fats The majority of these are solid at room temperature. They are linked with raising the level of cholesterol in the blood, which causes the arteries to clog up, thus narrowing them and eventually stopping the blood from being able to flow freely to the heart, resulting in a heart attack. Butter and cocoa butter are high in saturated fat.

Unsaturated fats These can be either mono-unsaturated, as found in olive oil, or polyunsaturated, found in seed and vegetable oils, oily fish and nuts; they do not raise blood cholesterol.

Vitamins These are valuable for boosting the body's immunity and encouraging healing. They are loosely divided into two groups.

Water-soluble vitamins (B group and vitamin C) These cannot be stored in the body, so need to be supplied by our diet on a daily basis. One of the roles of vitamin C is to help the body absorb iron – hence, drinking a glass of orange juice at breakfast time will mean that the maximum use is made of the iron in breakfast cereals.

Fat-soluble vitamins (vitamins A, D, E and K) As the term suggests, these vitamins are found in foods rich in fat. They can be stored by the body and, consequently, do not necessarily need to be ingested daily. Hence it is important, if taking supplements, to adhere to the correct dosage, and to take into account how much fat-soluble vitamins you are also getting from your diet, to avoid a build up.

Minerals Like vitamins, minerals are only needed in very small quantities and are necessary to help maintain the body. Calcium is one of the most notable: found in dairy products, it is essential for strong bones and teeth. Iron helps prevent anaemia.

It is difficult to give accurate amounts of exactly how much each person should consume, as many factors make our needs different. There are, however, generally accepted guidelines published by the Food Standards Agency, which we can use as the basis for our understanding of good nutritional practice, tweaking them according to our body's individual requirements. By categorising basic nutrients into the food groups that are rich in them, we can develop some general plans for how much of each we should consume.

BASIC FOOD GROUPS

Bread, potatoes, rice, cereals, pasta, oats When unrefined, these contain complex carbohydrates, which fill us up by bulking out our food. They are also rich in the B group of vitamins and whole grains are a good source of fibre.

Fruit and vegetables These are especially rich in vitamins and minerals, as well as being good sources of fibre and containing hardly any fat. Many are also rich in antioxidants, which are thought to play a role in protecting against some cancers and heart disease. It is currently recommended that we eat at least five portions of fruit and vegetables each day, and preferably a wide variety. Aim for a mix of colours and you should achieve this!

Dairy products, such as milk, cheese, cream and yogurt Dairy products are excellent sources of calcium and some fat-soluble vitamins. They also contribute some protein. However, because their fat is of the saturated kind, it is advisable to limit the amount of them in the diet and substitute lower-fat alternatives where possible.

Meat, fish, eggs, pulses and lentils These are primarily the protein group, needed for growth and repair of the body's tissues and cells. The amount needed varies according to age, whether we are male or female, and how active a lifestyle we have.

Butter, margarine, oils, sugar and foods high in these substances This group should form the smallest part of our diet, since fat provides double the calories of carbohydrates or proteins and sugars provide only calories, with no nutritional benefit whatsoever.

Margarines have proven to be quite a challenge to identify under one umbrella – such is the extent of the range now available: low-fat alternatives; margarines high in polyunsaturates and mono-unsaturates; and those that actively lower your cholesterol level; organic varieties; and margarine for vegan diets – all endeavour to meet our needs, and provide a seemingly endless variety.

All the recipes in this book have been tested using a reduced-fat butter spread, made by a famous Danish company. Butter or margarine can be used instead; however, if using margarine, it is vital to check that its fat content makes it suitable for baking with, as many low-fat spreads do not have enough oil in them to stabilise them when heated.

It will depend on your own family's needs and beliefs, as to which you choose. Butter is high in saturated fat but, on the other hand, it is a pure substance with very few additives, and low-fat and reduced-salt versions are available. Margarines (which are high in polyunsaturates and mono-unsaturates) on the other hand, tend to be better for the heart, but contain a wealth of E-numbers in terms of colourings, flavourings, preservatives and emulsifiers. It may well be that you decide to use a combination in order to reap the benefits which they each have, and this is really the crux of this book – to be able to make the right choices for you, from what is on offer.

Sugar is devoid of nutrients. As many foods naturally contain sugar it is worthwhile getting into the habit of tasting first to see if you do in fact need to add any at all, or just a little. Unrefined brown sugars bring a different spectrum of flavours to a recipe, their strength depending on the degree of molasses which they contain.

A WORD ON FIBRE

Food has become more and more processed over the centuries and the result of this refining is that, in the case of whole grains, much of the outer husk is removed to produce white flour and white rice. This process drastically depletes the fibre content, as well as removing some of the valuable B-group of vitamins contained in the husk. Fibre is important to alleviate constipation by adding bulk to food, which accelerates the movement of digested food through the large intestine. Getting enough fibre in your diet helps to reduce bowel disorders and guard against cancers in this region.

SALT IN THE DIET

Further research is needed on the effect of salt on the body, but it has been linked to heart disease, strokes and raised blood pressure in some people. Ways of reducing salt intake include eating less crisps and nuts, not automatically adding salt in cooking and on the plate and seasoning food with herbs and spices instead. Processed foods are often particularly high in salt, whereas home-cooked food gives you control of the amount of salt you eat. Potassium reduces the effect of the sodium in salt, helping to counteract high blood pressure and the risk of strokes. Foods high in potassium include potatoes, bananas and dried apricots.

To summarise, a healthy diet should contain a limited amount of saturated fat, sugar and salt, whilst still containing foods that provide protein, complex carbohydrates, vitamins, minerals and fibre. To ensure that we have a well balanced diet, we need to eat a wide selection of foods.

In this country, we are lucky enough to be able to eat for pleasure as well as to satisfy hunger, choosing – from an amazingly wide selection of foods – those that we particularly like. We can, quite literally, 'have our cake and eat it'. Research, notably on rising obesity in adults and children directly related to diet and exercise, shows that we are somewhat overwhelmed by our choice! *Healthy Fast Food* sets out to make the best use of the choices we have, consciously deciding how we can avoid eating too many fatty, salty or sugary foods. The recipes in this book will help you to do just that.

HEALTHY SHOPPING

FARMERS' MARKETS

Together with farm shops and box schemes, which deliver weekly supplies of organically grown foods, these markets are becoming increasingly popular around the country, in a bid to slow the drastic industrialisation of the food industry. Their common denominator is that the produce is all locally grown and, more often than not, by farmers who are discriminating in use of their fertilisers and pesticides and concerned for the humane husbandry of their animals. These outlets have other beneficial spin-offs: they use less packaging, strengthen links between urban and rural communities, use less fuel for transport (aeroplanes and lorries are not an issue here); consequently, moreover, they offer fresher food. They encourage us to eat more as nature intended, fruit and vegetables in season, and all the more precious for their limited availability. Since their final destination is close to hand, fresh produce can be picked when fully ripe – so it reaches the consumer at its peak in terms of vitamin content and taste, before, particularly in the case of vegetables, the natural sugars all change to starch. The fresher and better the quality of the food, the simpler the cooking method should be: each ingredient should stand on its own, rather than having its flavour 'pepped up'. Quite often, eating well is eating simply.

ORGANIC FARMING

Organic farming has, as its central concern, the possible effects of chemical residues from intensive farming methods on humans and the environment. It has come a long way over the past few years. In response to consumers' wishes, supermarkets themselves now devote ever-increasing aisle space to organic fruit and vegetables in particular, as well as a general range of organic products.

The principles of organic farming decree the use of organic fertilisers, which are less harmful to wildlife than inorganic (chemical-based) ones; crop rotation, so that the earth is not stripped of its nutrients; and cattle, pigs, hens and sheep that are allowed to roam on grassland, fed organic fodder, not given growth promoters and only treated with antibiotics if there is a medical need.

Organic dairy produce has a fuller flavour – the animal's milk reflecting the quality of its fodder. Organic meat has had longer to develop naturally, resulting in meat which melts in the mouth. Organically grown crops contain fewer chemical residues (which cannot be washed off by scrubbing – a particular concern with fruit and vegetables) which can be absorbed into our bodies. Organically grown fruit and vegetables have a superior flavour to their mass-produced supermarket counterparts, since they are allowed to ripen naturally before being picked. This makes them a richer source of vitamins, which are at their peak when the fruit ripens.

HEALTHY COOKING TECHNIQUES

We must not negate the benefits of buying healthy food by cooking it unhealthily. Careful consideration should be given, in particular, to finding alternatives to frying.

Grilling and *baking* are obvious options. *Griddling* – a fast form of cooking at a high temperature with minimum or no fat added – is kind on calories and seals in the flavour.

Steaming is a good choice for vegetables containing water-soluble vitamins, because it minimises the loss that inevitably occurs during boiling. If you do boil vegetables, do it in the minimum amount of water, without salt, for a short length of time.

Vegetables and fruit start to lose vitamins as soon as they are cut and exposed to the air, due to oxidation; so they should be prepared immediately before cooking. Many nutrients lie just below the skin of fruit and vegetables so, if possible, just wash or scrub before using.

HEALTHY ALTERNATIVES

Below are some healthy substitutes for unhealthy foods that can easily be incorporated into your daily diet.
Sugary drinks Use natural fruit juices.
Cream Substitute yogurt. 'Live' or 'bio' yogurt contains live bacteria that help maintain a healthy balance in the gut, counteracting the bacteria that can cause thrush, diarrhoea, irritable bowel syndrome and constipation. Looking after the bowel therefore assists the immune system. Take care when using in cooking, though, as low-fat yogurt will curdle if boiled.
Dairy products Look for lower-/reduced-fat alternatives, for example, semi-skimmed milk, and half fat crème fraîche.
Cheese Using strongly flavoured cheeses, such as Cheddar and Parmesan, means that you need less to achieve a good flavour.
Jam Replace with high-fruit-content spread or no-added-sugar jam.
Free-range eggs Preferable to those from battery or caged animals, because the hens are well looked after and this is reflected in the colour of the egg yolks, and their flavour.
Meat Butchers have reacted to the call from the public for leaner cuts of meat. When buying sausages, for example, check that they contain a relatively high percentage of meat.

We are fortunate enough to have all the necessary resources at our disposal to enjoy a perfectly balanced diet – hence the breadth of this book, from salads with low-calorie dressings to cakes such as brownies using natural, wholesome ingredients, free from artificial colours and preservatives. Whether your interest lies in becoming more aware of the food you eat, and what it contains; in using fresh ingredients for the best flavour; or because your weekdays are so full that it is a treat at the weekend to have the time to spend on preparing home-made food – and all the therapeutic value which this in itself brings – there is something in this book for everyone. We, as a family, have never eaten as well, and as a result, felt so good for it, as when testing these recipes. I hope that you will enjoy them as well, and take a fresh look at what you eat!

How fitting that this book on healthy eating should start off with a chapter containing vegetables as the main ingredient in each recipe! This chapter is a celebration of vegetables — their vibrancy of colour, breadth of textures and diverseness of flavours.

Home-made soups cannot be rivalled by processed, canned and packet equivalents. Soups you make yourself are far more nutritious, superior in flavour and cheaper to make, and you will often have enough left over for another day.

SOUPS & SALADS

Salads can be served as accompaniments (Sunflower & Sultana Coleslaw, page 16) or as main courses in themselves (Warm Chilli Beef Salad, page 20). The choice of salads on offer at supermarkets and takeaway sandwich bars is fairly predictable and limited, and they are often made with synthetic, calorie-laden dressings. Making your own will give you the peace of mind of knowing not just that everything has been hygienically prepared but also exactly what has gone into the salad and dressing. Salads are so flexible that, in terms of choice, this chapter barely represents the tip of the iceberg!

SERVES: 4–6
PREPARATION & COOKING TIME:
35 minutes + 20 minutes cooking
FREEZING: RECOMMENDED

PER SERVING (x 4): 255 calories, 13 g fat

1 tablespoon olive oil
115 g (4 oz) pancetta or rindless back bacon,
snipped into pieces
1 leek, sliced finely
1 carrot, diced
1 celery stick, sliced finely
1 large onion, chopped finely
400 g can of chopped tomatoes
1.4 litres (2½ pints) good-quality vegetable,
ham or chicken stock
1 bay leaf
1 tablespoon tomato purée
½ x 410 g can of cannellini or butter beans,
rinsed and drained
50 g (2 oz) small pasta, e.g. conchigliette
a handful of fresh basil leaves, torn roughly
175 g (6 oz) Savoy cabbage or
spring greens, shredded
sea salt and freshly ground black pepper

finely grated Parmesan cheese,
to garnish (optional)

This **timeless Italian soup** is packed with goodness, probably providing at least two out of the five recommended daily portions of fruit and vegetables. Adding the cabbage right at the end ensures that it keeps its lovely green colour.

Vary the vegetables according to the season – for instance, substitute courgettes or spinach for the cabbage during the summer months. All the minerals and vitamins that seep out of the vegetables during cooking are retained in the soup's liquid, together with their flavours.

1   Heat the oil in a large pan. Add the pancetta or bacon, leek, carrot, celery and onion. Toss them in the oil, cover pan with a lid and leave to 'sweat', over a low heat, for 10 minutes, without browning. Shake the pan occasionally.
2   Add the tomatoes, stock, bay leaf and tomato purée. Bring to the boil, cover, and simmer for 20 minutes.
3   Add the beans, pasta and basil. Season and return to the boil. Simmer for another 10 minutes, or until the pasta is cooked.
4   Three minutes before the end of the cooking time, add the cabbage to the pan, cover, and allow it to steam on top of the soup.
5   Stir through the cabbage and serve.

COOK'S NOTE: Minestrone is usually finished off with a generous topping of grated Parmesan. Personally, I feel that this rather 'takes over' from the subtle flavour of the vegetables. As a compromise, hand round a bowl of freshly grated Parmesan for those who feel that the soup needs it.

MINESTRONE SOUP

SERVES: 4
PREPARATION & COOKING TIME:
20 minutes + 20 minutes cooking
FREEZING: recommended

HOT TOMATO SOUP

This fresh soup is very quick to make and has a **brilliant red colour** – all natural! The little bit of chilli gives it a **warming glow**. Do take care to wash your hands thoroughly after handling chillies, though. If you wish, serve garnished with basil or chopped parsley and accompany with a cheesy bread.

PER SERVING: 71 calories, 4 g fat

1 tablespoon olive oil
1 onion, chopped
1 carrot, sliced
$^1/_2$ fat red chilli, de-seeded and chopped finely
400 g can of chopped tomatoes
about 600 ml (1 pint) good vegetable, ham or chicken stock
1 bay leaf
$^1/_2$ teaspoon brown sugar
sea salt and freshly ground black pepper

1 Heat the oil in a saucepan. Stir in the onion, carrot and chilli. Cover the pan and leave the vegetables to 'sweat', over a low heat, for 5 minutes, without browning. Shake the pan occasionally.
2 Add the tomatoes with their juice, stock, bay leaf and sugar. Season to taste. Bring to the boil, reduce the heat, cover and simmer for 20 minutes, until the vegetables are cooked.
3 Allow the soup to cool slightly. Remove the bay leaf, pour into a blender and liquidise until smooth. Add a little more stock, if necessary, to achieve the required consistency.
4 Rinse out the pan. Return the soup to the hob and heat through gently, without boiling. Check the seasoning and serve.

SERVES: 4–6
PREPARATION: 15 minutes
FREEZING: not recommended

SUNFLOWER & SULTANA COLESLAW

This fromage frais based coleslaw is a million miles away from the rich, mayonnaise laden pots that you would buy at a supermarket, and yet is so **quick and simple to make** – doubly so if you possess a food processor. The sultanas add fibre and a delicious sweetness. Sunflower seeds are rich in protein and fibre, adding texture and flavour as well – sprinkle them in just before serving for maximum 'bite'.

PER SERVING: 212 calories, 16 g fat

FOR THE DRESSING:
200 g tub of fromage frais
2 tablespoons cider vinegar
1 teaspoon Dijon mustard
4 tablespoons olive oil
$^1/_2$ teaspoon sugar
sea salt and freshly ground black pepper

FOR THE SALAD:
225 g (8 oz) white cabbage, shredded finely
1 carrot, weighing about 115 g (4 oz), grated finely
$^1/_2$ small red onion, chopped very finely
50 g (2 oz) sultanas
3 tablespoons sunflower seeds, toasted

1 For the dressing, combine the fromage frais, cider vinegar and mustard in a small bowl. Gradually whisk in the oil and season to taste with sugar and a little salt and pepper.
2 In a larger bowl, mix together cabbage, carrot, onion and sultanas. Pour over the dressing and mix well to combine. Toss in the sunflower seeds just before serving.

SERVES: 4
PREPARATION & COOKING TIME:
15 minutes + 30 minutes soaking + 25 minutes cooking
FREEZING: not recommended

'CREAM' OF MUSHROOM SOUP

'Bye bye' canned mushroom soup! Porcini mushrooms give this **home-made version a depth of flavour**, which surpasses the dehydrated packet or canned types. Mushrooms are a particularly rich source of some of the B-group of vitamins. If you wish to cut down on calories then omit the crème fraîche.

PER SERVING: 105 calories, 8 g fat

15 g (¹/₂ oz) dried porcini mushrooms
1 tablespoon olive oil
1 large onion, chopped finely
225 g (8 oz) flat mushrooms, wiped, halved and sliced
1 garlic clove, crushed
850 ml (1¹/₂ pints) vegetable stock
sea salt and freshly ground black pepper
4 tablespoons half-fat crème fraîche, to serve
chopped fresh parsley, to garnish

1 Place the porcini mushrooms in a smallish bowl; pour over 150 ml (¹/₄ pint) of warm water, and leave to soak for 30 minutes.
2 In a large pan, heat the oil and sauté the onion for 10 minutes, until softened.
3 Add the soaked mushrooms with the soaking liquid, sliced flat mushrooms, garlic, stock and seasoning. Bring to the boil, reduce the heat, cover and simmer for 15 minutes.
4 Cool the soup a little and reserve a few of the mushrooms. Liquidise the remainder to give a smooth soup.
5 Rinse out the pan. Return the soup to the hob and heat through gently, without boiling. Pour into individual serving bowls. Spoon a tablespoon of crème fraîche in the middle of each. Place a couple of mushroom slices on top and sprinkle with a little chopped parsley.

SERVES: 4–6
PREPARATION TIME: 10 minutes
FREEZING: not recommended

CRANBERRY, BLUE CHEESE, PEAR & WALNUT SALAD

The idea for this salad was given to me by my friend Issie, now living near New York, where a well-known chain of coffee bars sell a version of it. Cranberries, native to North America, are now more widely available over here (if all other avenues fail, try a health food shop for dried ones) and a good source of fibre and vitamin C. This is a winter salad – the dark green salad leaves and red, berry-like cranberries are reminiscent of holly. Delicious with ham and Stilton at Christmas time, although I prefer the creamy, softness of Saint Agur.

PER SERVING: 285 calories, 22 g fat

FOR THE DRESSING:
$^1/_4$ teaspoon English mustard powder
$^1/_4$ teaspoon soft brown sugar
$1^1/_2$ teaspoons balsamic vinegar
$1^1/_2$ teaspoons white wine vinegar
1 tablespoon extra virgin olive oil
1 tablespoon sunflower or vegetable oil
sea salt and freshly ground black pepper

FOR THE SALAD:
120 g bag of salad leaves, including red chard or red beet
115 g (4 oz) Saint Agur, dolcelatte or Stilton
40 g ($1^1/_2$ oz) walnut pieces
40 g ($1^1/_2$ oz) dried cranberries
1 large, ripe Comice pear

1 Place the mustard, sugar, salt, pepper and vinegars in a bowl. Mix together. Gradually whisk in the oils.
2 Put the salad leaves in a serving bowl. Cube or crumble the cheese into bite-sized pieces and add to the salad, with the walnut pieces and cranberries.
3 Wash the pear and, leaving its skin on, core and thinly slice. Stir into the dressing to coat it thoroughly.
4 Just before serving, add the pear and dressing to the salad and toss well.

SERVES: 4
PREPARATION & COOKING TIME:
30 minutes
FREEZING: not recommended

PER SERVING: 209 calories, 10 g fat

Somewhat of a paradox of a title for this Thai-style main-course salad, packed with plenty of vegetables! It makes a **wonderful informal supper party recipe,** as all the preparation can be done in advance and, because it is equally good warm or cold, an exact serving schedule is not necessary.

Chicken could equally well be used instead of beef, if you prefer. In the absence of pak-choi, spinach is an excellent substitute, but stir this in at step 5 rather than 4.

WARM CHILLI BEEF SALAD

1 Whisk together all the dressing ingredients, and set on one side.
2 Bring a pan of water to the boil. Break the rice noodles into three sections. Add to the water, making sure that they are fully immersed. Cover the pan, turn off the heat, and leave for 4 minutes. Drain and toss the noodles in the dressing.
3 In a wok, heat the oil until hot. Stir in the pepper, chilli, garlic and ginger. Stir-fry for 1 minute, moving the ingredients around the pan the whole time.
4 Add the steak and pak choi and cook for a further 2–3 minutes.
5 Remove the pan from the heat and stir in the mushrooms, carrot, spring onions, coriander and noodles. Mix well and serve warm.

FOR THE DRESSING:
2 tablespoons reduced-salt soy sauce
2 teaspoons sesame oil
2 teaspoons sweet chilli sauce
juice of 1/2 lime
freshly ground black pepper

FOR THE SALAD:
115 g (4 oz) stir-fry rice noodles
1 tablespoon sunflower or vegetable oil
1/2 red pepper, de-seeded and sliced thinly
1 red chilli, de-seeded and chopped finely
1 garlic clove, crushed
1 teaspoon grated fresh root ginger
**200 g (7 oz) sirloin steak, fat trimmed,
   cut into very thin strips**
1 head of pak choi, quartered and rinsed
**115 g (4 oz) baby button mushrooms, wiped
and halved**
**1 carrot, scrubbed and cut into matchstick-
size batons**
1 bunch of spring onions, sliced thinly
**2 rounded tablespoons chopped fresh
coriander**

SERVES: 4
PREPARATION TIME:
15 minutes + at least 1 hour standing
FREEZING: not recommended

PER SERVING: 225 calories, 14 g fat

This is not a palate-blowing concoction but more of a **warming, satisfying** one, with tangy flavours that mellow overnight once the beans have had a chance to absorb the spices in its dressing. This makes it a good choice when entertaining, as it **actually benefits from being prepared in advance**. (Remember to wash your hands well after handling the chilli.)

Beans are an excellent source of protein and fibre, as well as being low in fat. They also depend on having some added salt to bring out their flavour, so I would recommend its use here.

MEXICAN BEAN SALAD

1   Firstly make the dressing. Dry-fry the spices by placing the paprika, cumin and chilli powder in a small frying pan. Cook over a low heat for 1–2 minutes, just to release their flavour. Watch them like a hawk, as they tend to burn easily. (Your sense of smell will tell you when they are ready!)

2   Place the cooked spices in a small mixing bowl. Pound the garlic to a purée with a little sea salt and add, with the lime juice and oregano. Gradually whisk in the oil and sugar.

3   Combine all the salad ingredients in a serving dish, pour over the dressing and stir well to combine. Set aside for at least an hour, longer if possible, to allow the flavours to develop.

FOR THE DRESSING:
$1/2$ **teaspoon paprika**
$1/4$ **teaspoon ground cumin**
$1/8$ **teaspoon mild chilli powder**
1 small garlic clove, peeled
juice of $1/2$ **lime**
$1/8$ **teaspoon dried oregano**
$1 1/2$ **tablespoons sunflower oil**
$1/4$ **teaspoon brown sugar**
coarse sea salt

FOR THE SALAD:
420 g can of borlotti or mixed beans, rinsed and drained
$1/2$ **orange, red or yellow pepper, de-seeded and diced**
1 ripe tomato, skinned, de-seeded and chopped
$1/2$ **bunch of spring onions, sliced**
$1/2$ **fat red chilli, de-seeded and chopped very finely (wear rubber gloves to protect your hands)**
1 ripe avocado, halved, stone removed and flesh diced
1 rounded tablespoon chopped fresh coriander

PREPARATION & COOKING TIME:
20 minutes + 20 minutes standing + cooling
FREEZING: not recommended

PER SERVING: 218 calories, 11 g fat

This salad is **extremely versatile** because you can also serve it warm — it goes particularly well with lamb, grilled or casseroled. It keeps well, too. If making a day in advance, then prepare to the end of step 3. Adding the herbs and pine nuts on the day ensures that the herbs keep their **fresh greenness** and the nuts their bite.

MOROCCAN COUSCOUS SALAD

225 g (8 oz) couscous
2 rounded tablespoons sultanas
3 tablespoons extra virgin olive oil
1 large onion, chopped
1/4 teaspoon each paprika, ground cumin,
ground ginger and ground cinnamon
1/8 teaspoon cayenne pepper
1/4 teaspoon coarse sea salt, ground
juice of 1 small lemon
2 rounded tablespoons each chopped fresh
mint and parsley
2 tablespoons pine nuts, toasted

1 Place the couscous and sultanas in a bowl and pour over 300 ml (1/2 pint) of boiling water. Cover with a clean tea towel and leave to stand for 20 minutes, until all the water has been absorbed.

2 Meanwhile, heat 1 tablespoon of the oil in a frying pan. Add the onion and fry until soft and golden. Stir in the spices and cayenne and cook for 1 minute.

3 Add the salt to the couscous and fork through, to separate the grains. Stir in the remaining olive oil and the lemon juice. Leave to cool completely before adding the spicy onion mixture.

4 Just prior to serving, mix in the chopped mint and parsley with the toasted pine nuts.

Dips and sauces have been a fast-growing area on the supermarket shelves, whether they are processed and bottled or sold 'fresh' from the chiller cabinet. In response to public demand low-fat alternatives are now available. Whichever way you look at it, though, they all contain a long list of additives. Making your own dips and sauces eliminates the need for all of these – the flavour is far superior, they are freshly made, do not need unnatural colours, and, particularly in the case of Tomato Salsa (page 26) and Tzatziki (page 24), retain the crisp texture of the vegetables.

DIPS & SAUCES

The recipes in this chapter are predominantly low in fat and, for those which traditionally tend to be high in calories, I have used low-fat alternatives, such as ricotta cheese and natural yogurt for Roasted Garlic & Chive Dip (page 26) and fromage frais in place of mayonnaise in the Marie-Rose Sauce (page 25).

Home-made sauces cost far less than bought ones and Barbecue Sauce (page 28) and Tomato Ketchup (page 30) make use of ingredients which you will probably have to hand in your storecupboard anyway. The majority of recipes in this chapter are very quick to make, taking less than 5 minutes, and are so easy that you'll not need to buy another sauce again!

MAKES: 425 ml (³/₄ pint)
PREPARATION TIME:
5 minutes + at least 1 hour chilling
FREEZING: not recommended

MAKES: 150 ml (¹/₄ pint)
PREPARATION TIME:
10 minutes + 1 hour chilling
FREEZING: not recommended

HOUMOUS

TZATZIKI

It is not often that you can conjure up such **a delicious recipe so quickly**. This dip has the added benefit of being nutritious into the bargain – chick-peas being a good source of fibre and rich in protein. Houmous is a subtle creamy colour, with a refreshing, tangy taste. Serve as an accompaniment to Lamb Kebabs (page 37) or as a dip with pitta bread and crudités of red pepper strips, mange tout and batons of carrots.

PER RECIPE: 279 calories, 16 g fat

420 g can of chick-peas, rinsed and drained
3 tablespoons natural low-fat 'bio' yogurt
1 small garlic clove, crushed
2 tablespoons extra virgin olive oil
1 tablespoon lemon juice
sea salt and freshly ground black pepper

1   Place all the ingredients in a blender and liquidise until the mixture runs smoothly.
2   Adjust the seasoning to taste and turn into a bowl. Cover and chill in the fridge for at least an hour, to give the flavours a chance to mingle.

There is a very fine divide between this **classic Greek dish**, and the Indian raita, which has added mint. Whereas the Greek version is used as a dip for *mezzes*, raita is traditionally served to temper a spicy dish, that is, take away some of its palate-burning heat! Tzatziki does not keep well, so use within a few hours of preparing.

PER RECIPE: 300 calories, 22 g fat

¹/₂ cucumber, wiped
200 g tub of Greek yogurt
1 small garlic clove, crushed
sea salt and freshly ground black pepper

1   Coarsely grate the cucumber, leaving the skin on. Place in a sieve and extract as much of the liquid as you can, using the back of a wooden spoon. Then wrap the shredded cucumber in a clean tea towel and squeeze out any remaining juice.
2   In a small bowl, mix together the yogurt and garlic. Stir in the grated cucumber and season with salt and pepper to taste. Cover and refrigerate for an hour before serving.

MAKES: 300 ml (½ pint)
PREPARATION TIME: 5 minutes
FREEZING: not recommended

MAKES: about 225 ml (8 fl oz)
PREPARATION TIME:
less than 5 minutes! + 1 hour chilling
FREEZING: not recommended

MILD CURRY SAUCE

This is a **beautifully coloured sauce**, ideal for use with cold chicken for a summer buffet dish. It's loosely based on the sauce invented to celebrate the coronation of Queen Elizabeth II but I have substituted yogurt for the traditionally used cream and low-fat mayonnaise for the full-fat version. Using curry paste rather than powder eliminates the need to cook the sauce at all. This quantity is sufficient to coat the meat from a medium-sized cooked chicken.

PER RECIPE: 668 calories, 54 g fat

1 tablespoon medium curry paste
1 rounded tablespoon mango chutney
150 ml (¼ pint) reduced-fat mayonnaise
150 ml (¼ pint) natural 'bio' yogurt
1 tablespoon lemon juice

1   In a smallish bowl, combine the curry paste and mango chutney.
2   Blend in the mayonnaise and then the yogurt. Mix until smooth.
3   Stir in the lemon juice. Refrigerate until required.

MARIE-ROSE SAUCE

This sauce is, traditionally, mayonnaise-based but if you use fromage frais the **fat content is reduced by about 60 per cent**. Spooned over prawns, this makes a lovely filling for jacket potatoes, or a sauce for prawn cocktail.

PER RECIPE: 279 calories, 16 g fat

200 g tub of fromage frais
2 teaspoons tomato purée
2 teaspoons lemon juice
1 teaspoon Worcestershire sauce
1 teaspoon creamed horseradish sauce
a pinch of soft brown sugar
freshly ground black pepper

1   Beat together all the ingredients in a bowl, until thoroughly combined.
2   Chill for at least an hour to give the flavours a chance to mingle.

SERVES: 4
PREPARATION TIME: 15 minutes + 1 hour standing
FREEZING: not recommended

MAKES: 300 ml (1/2 pint)
PREPARATION & COOKING TIME:
10 minutes + 30 minutes cooking + chilling
FREEZING: not recommended

TOMATO SALSA

ROASTED GARLIC & CHIVE DIP

This just looks so healthy, and equally importantly, tastes wonderful. **Visually vibrant**, with its red, purple and green colours, the addition of lime juice and chilli makes the flavour 'zing'. Home-prepared salsa is a million miles away from its shop-bought counterpart – a sludgy, soft mass. Salsa's strong taste does tend to dominate, though, so serve it alongside less distinctive food, which it will complement, rather than compete with. It makes a delicious accompaniment to the Home-made Quarter Pounders (page 61) and would go equally well with grilled white fish or meat. Alternatively, serve as a dip with tortilla chips to scoop it up. Salsa is best eaten fresh, so aim to prepare it only a couple of hours before serving.

PER RECIPE: 106 calories, 1 g fat

4 large ripe tomatoes (vine-ripened ones are best)
1/2 red onion, chopped very finely
2 fat green chillies, de-seeded and chopped very finely
2 tablespoons chopped fresh coriander
juice of 1 lime
a pinch of sugar
sea salt and freshly ground black pepper

1 Wash and dry the tomatoes. Quarter, remove core and seeds and chop the flesh finely.
2 Place in a bowl, with the red onion, chillies and coriander.
3 Stir in the lime juice and season with the sugar and salt and pepper to taste. Mix well to combine and set aside for an hour, to allow the flavours to mingle.

Garlic, when roasted, undergoes some kind of metamorphosis, resulting in a **divinely pungent, creamy taste**. Garlic itself has long been used in herbal medicine for its health benefits – particularly in protecting the immune system by encouraging the body to release anti-infection cells. So this makes an ideal choice for wintertime. Dips are notoriously high in fat so this low-fat alternative makes a welcome change. Serve with a rainbow of mixed vegetable crudités or wedges (page 58).

PER RECIPE: 301 calories, 17 g fat

1 head of garlic
olive oil, for brushing
1/2 x 250 g tub of ricotta cheese
150 ml (1/4 pint) low-fat natural 'bio' yogurt
1 tablespoon very finely chopped fresh chives
freshly ground black pepper

1 Preheat the oven to Gas Mark 6/electric oven 200°C/fan oven 180°C.
2 Place the whole head of garlic in a roasting dish and brush with a little oil, to prevent it from burning. Cook towards the top of the oven for about 30 minutes. Test that the flesh is ready by inserting a sharp knife into the cloves, the pulp should be soft. Leave to cool.
3 Separate the garlic into individual cloves and, holding the pointed end, squeeze the soft, creamy flesh out of the skin. Pound to a paste with a pestle and mortar.
4 Beat together the ricotta and yogurt. Stir in the puréed garlic and chives. Season to taste with pepper and chill prior to serving.

MAKES 150 ml (¹/₄ pint)
PREPARATION & COOKING TIME:
5 minutes + 20 minutes cooking
FREEZING: recommended

MAKES: 425 ml (³/₄ pint)
PREPARATION: 15 minutes + 30 minutes standing
FREEZING: not recommended

BARBECUE SAUCE

GUACAMOLE

This sauce really only involves a little stirring and has a real 'kick'. Most of the ingredients will probably be in your storecupboard anyway – far quicker than having to trek to the shops – and far fewer E-numbers! Use it to brush over spare ribs or chicken drumsticks before grilling, and watch the moisture evaporate to give an **irresistible sticky result**. This sauce can also be served as a dip with crisp Cos lettuce leaves (the colour contrast is spectacular!), or drain a can of mixed beans and combine to make a spicy bean feast.

This traditional Mexican dip is widely available in supermarkets, a velvety, bright green concoction that is far away from the **'zingy'**, **chunky, home-made version**. Do not prepare too far in advance, though, as the avocado tends to turn slightly brown on standing.

After years of experiencing disappointing avocados, whose ripening timetable was invariably out of sync with my entertaining one, the discovery of supermarket 'ripe and ready to eat' fruit has ensured success every time – perfect texture, together with maximum flavour.

PER RECIPE: 284 calories, 16 g fat

PER RECIPE: 624 calories, 59 g fat

1 garlic clove, crushed
2 tablespoons tomato purée
2 tablespoons clear honey
1 tablespoon white wine vinegar
1 tablespoon reduced-salt soy sauce
1 tablespoon olive oil
1 teaspoon English mustard powder
¹/₂ teaspoon dried thyme
Tabasco sauce

2 ripe avocados
juice of 1 lime
2 ripe tomatoes, skinned, de-seeded and chopped finely
¹/₂ small red onion, grated
1 small garlic clove, crushed
1 fat green chilli, de-seeded and chopped very finely
2 tablespoons chopped fresh coriander
a pinch of sugar
sea salt

1 In a small saucepan, combine the garlic, tomato purée, honey, vinegar, soy sauce, oil, mustard and thyme. Blend in 150 ml (¹/₄ pint) of water.
2 Bring to the boil, reduce the heat and simmer, uncovered, for 15–20 minutes, until the sauce reduces slightly and thickens a little.
3 Strain through a sieve. Add a few drops of Tabasco to taste. Use hot or cold.

1 Halve the avocados and remove the stones. Scoop out the flesh into a bowl, making sure that you include the greenest part nearest the skin. Pour over the lime juice and mash well, using a fork. You should end up with a slightly lumpy mixture.
2 Stir in the remaining ingredients and season to taste with sugar and salt.
3 It is exposure to air that causes avocado to brown, so cover with cling film, ensuring that it actually touches the guacamole's surface. Leave to stand for half an hour to allow the flavours time to mingle.
4 Serve with crisp sticks of raw vegetables and strips of pitta bread. Any left over should be stored in the fridge, but will tend to discolour.

SERVES: 4–6
PREPARATION & COOKING TIME:
25 minutes + 50 minutes cooking
FREEZING: recommended

BOLOGNESE SAUCE

This is not a true ragù sauce, as I have 'bumped up' the vegetable content by adding extra carrots and leeks. In addition to helping **boost your daily fresh vegetable intake**, this is an ideal way of ensuring that children who are not keen on vegetables increase their consumption, without even realising.

I have used steak mince, which has a low fat content (around 7 per cent). Generally, price is a good indicator for choosing healthier meat – the more expensive the cut, the leaner the meat! This sauce is traditionally served with spaghetti or other pasta, topped with grated Parmesan cheese.

PER RECIPE: 986 calories, 25 g fat

450 g (1 lb) minced steak or lean mince
3 rashers unsmoked back bacon, chopped
1 onion, chopped finely
1 carrot, chopped finely
1 leek, chopped finely
1 garlic clove, crushed
400 g can of chopped tomatoes
50 g (2 oz) flat mushrooms, wiped and sliced
150 ml (¼ pint) red wine
1 tablespoon tomato purée
2 tablespoons chopped fresh parsley
1 teaspoon dried oregano
1 bay leaf
a pinch of sugar
freshly ground black pepper

1 Heat a large pan. Add the mince, bacon, onion, carrot, leek and garlic. Cook over a high heat, stirring frequently to break up the mince, for 5 minutes, until the meat is browned.
2 Add the canned tomatoes to the pan, with the mushrooms, red wine, tomato purée and herbs. Season with the sugar and plenty of freshly ground black pepper. Bring to the boil, reduce the heat, and simmer, covered, for 30 minutes. Stir occasionally.
3 Remove the lid and bubble for a further 20 minutes to concentrate the sauce. Remove the bay leaf and adjust the seasoning to taste.

SERVES: 4
PREPARATION TIME:
less than 5 minutes! + 30 minutes standing
FREEZING: recommended

PER RECIPE: 52 calories, 0 g fat

This sauce takes next to **no time to knock up, using storecupboard ingredients.** It has a bit more of a 'kick' to it than bought ketchup, and no hidden additives, flavourings or preservatives. Delicious served with Home-made Quarter Pounders (page 61), Fish in Breadcrumbs (page 57), or Crispy Chicken Dippers (page 58).

TOMATO KETCHUP

2 tablespoons tomato purée
1 teaspoon white wine vinegar
1 teaspoon muscovado sugar
¹/₂ teaspoon paprika
¹/₈ teaspoon mild chilli powder
freshly ground black pepper

1 Combine all the ingredients in a small bowl.
2 Stir in 2 tablespoons of boiling water and mix well.
3 Leave to stand for at least 30 minutes, to give the flavours a chance to combine. Store in the refrigerator.

Lunchtime, the middle of a busy day, when hunger pangs that need to be satisfied urgently tend to strike, is often a time, when we reach for the nearest 'fill me up' foods. Unfortunately, these invariably contain excessive amounts of salt, calories and additives, which, combined with their lack of nutrients, makes them a bad choice to keep us going through the rest of the afternoon. After you have read this chapter there will be no excuse for not being able to come up with a healthy alternative! Plenty of fresh vegetables (Not Pot-noodles!,

FOOD ON THE MOVE

page 32) are the main feature here, together with ideas for packed lunches (Chicken Caesar Wrap, page 36 and Cornish Pasties, page 41) and quick answers for a light meal (Spanish Frittata, page 42).

The common denominator of the recipes lies in the use of fresh, wholesome ingredients to sustain, rather than just creating a temporary burst of energy (as sugary snacks tend to do), the effects of which fizzle out after a relatively short time.

SERVES: 4
PREPARATION & COOKING TIME:
30 minutes
FREEZING: not recommended

PER SERVING: 449 calories, 18 g fat

225 g (8 oz) fine dried egg noodles
2 tablespoons sunflower oil
1 red pepper, de-seeded and cut into chunks
1 bunch of spring onions, trimmed and
sliced into 2.5 cm (1 -inch) lengths
1 large red chilli, de-seeded
and chopped finely
1 garlic clove, crushed
1 teaspoon grated fresh root ginger
50 g (2 oz) cashew nuts
115 g (4 oz) broccoli florets, broken up small
225 g (8 oz) cooked king prawns
175 g (6 oz) chestnut mushrooms,
wiped and halved or quartered
50 g (2 oz) mange tout, halved
125 ml (4 fl oz) vegetable stock
2 teaspoons cornflour
1 tablespoon reduced-salt soy sauce
1 tablespoon dry sherry
2 teaspoons sesame oil

To me, this recipe epitomises what is at the heart of this book — the difference between manufactured and home-cooked food. In all areas — appearance, taste and nutritional value — **this recipe is a world apart** from the ubiquitous tub of dehydrated, synthetic pot- noodles found on the shop shelf. And because stir-frying is so quick, most of the precious vitamins in the vegetables are preserved.

1 Cook the noodles in a pan of boiling water for 3 minutes. Drain and set aside.
2 Heat the sunflower oil in a wok. Add the red pepper, spring onions, chilli, garlic, ginger and cashew nuts. Stir-fry for 1 minute, keeping the ingredients moving all the time.
3 Add the broccoli and cook for a further minute.
4 Stir in the prawns, mushrooms, mange tout and stock. Stir-fry for 2 minutes.
5 Blend the cornflour with the soy sauce and sherry. Add to the pan with the cooked noodles, stirring all the time for about a minute, to thicken the sauce and heat through the noodles.
6 Stir in the sesame oil and serve at once, piled into individual bowls.

NOT POT-NOODLES!

SERVES: 4
PREPARATION & COOKING TIME:
15 minutes + 10 minutes cooking
FREEZING: not recommended

PER SERVING: 428 calories, 19 g fat

2 tablespoons sunflower or vegetable oil
1 bunch of spring onions
115 g (4 oz) button mushrooms,
wiped and sliced
450 g (1 lb) cooked basmati or fragrant rice,
approximately 200 g (7 oz) uncooked
weight, cooled and refrigerated
80 g (3 oz) frozen prawns, defrosted
1 small cooked chicken breast, weighing
about 80 g (3 oz), cubed
80 g (3 oz) dry-cured ham, cubed
80 g (3 oz) frozen peas, cooked
175 g (6 oz) beansprouts, rinsed
and patted dry
1 tablespoon reduced-salt soy sauce
1 teaspoon sesame oil

TO GARNISH:
1 teaspoon butter or margarine
2 eggs, lightly beaten
25 g (1 oz) shelled peanuts, chopped roughly

This **Chinese-style dish is a meal in itself**, packed with meat, fish, eggs and vegetables. I have used ham in place of pork but you could always add some pork tenderloin, cooked in the pan before adding the mushrooms and onion. Serve piled high in bowls.

1 Heat 1 tablespoon of oil in a non-stick wok or large frying pan. Reserve 2 spring onions, finely chop the remainder and add to the pan, with the mushrooms. Stir-fry for 2 minutes.
2 Add the remaining oil. Using a fork, break up the rice if lumpy. Add to pan with the prawns, chicken and ham. Cook gently for 5 minutes to heat through. Stir occasionally. Cover while you cook the garnish.
3 Heat half a teaspoon of the butter or margarine in an omelette pan. Pour in the eggs and cook for a couple of minutes until just set, and lightly browned underneath. Shred on a chopping board.
4 Add the remaining butter to the pan and brown the peanuts. Drain on kitchen paper.
5 Stir the peas, beansprouts, soy sauce and sesame oil into the rice mixture and heat through.
6 Finely shred the reserved spring onions. Pile the rice mixture into individual serving bowls. Top with strips of egg and spring onion. Finish with a sprinkling of peanuts.

EXTRA-SPECIAL FRIED RICE

SERVES: 4
PREPARATION & COOKING TIME:
30 minutes
FREEZING: not recommended

PER SERVING: 494 calories, 25 g fat

FOR THE STEAK:
2 teaspoons whole black peppercorns
350 g (12 oz) rump or sirloin steak,
trimmed of any excess fat
I garlic clove, crushed
I ½ tablespoons olive oil

FOR THE VEGETABLES:
I red pepper, de-seeded and sliced
into I cm (½ -inch) wide strips
I orange pepper, de-seeded and sliced into
I cm (½ -inch) wide strips
I red onion, sliced into thin wedges
I tablespoon olive oil

FOR THE DRESSING:
200 ml tub of half-fat crème fraîche
2 teaspoons finely chopped fresh chives

TO SERVE:
½ cos or romaine lettuce, shredded finely
4 wheat flour tortillas, 25 cm (10 inches)
in diameter

Making meat go further by adding vegetables is a good general healthy eating tip. These tortillas are a great choice for 'the boys' – a 'hefty' wrap, ideal for summertime, when you don't want to spend ages in the kitchen. Serve with Tomato Salsa (page 26). The steak can equally well be grilled; be sure to line the grill pan with foil for the vegetables.

1 Coarsely grind the peppercorns with a pestle and mortar. Press firmly into both sides of the steak.
2 Mix together the garlic and oil. Turn the steak in the mixture until thoroughly coated. Set to one side.
3 Combine the peppers and onion in a bowl. Drizzle with the oil and toss well.
4 Heat a griddle pan over a medium/high heat. Add the steak and cook for 2–3 minutes on each side. Remove from the pan and leave to stand while you prepare the rest of the ingredients. (This gives the juices a chance to be reabsorbed into the meat.)
5 Add the vegetables to the pan and cook for 5 minutes, until they have softened and are charred. Turn frequently.
6 Mix together the crème fraîche and chives.
7 Warm the tortillas as directed on the packet. Scatter the lettuce over the surfaces of each.
8 Thinly slice the steak and divide it between the tortillas. Distribute the vegetables and spoon the crème fraîche and chive sauce over each. Fold the bottom quarter of tortilla up, then each side in to enclose the filling. Serve at once.

PEPPERED STEAK TORTILLAS WITH CHARRED VEGETABLES

SERVES: 4
PREPARATION TIME: 15 minutes
FREEZING: not recommended

CHICKEN CAESAR WRAP

Caesar dressing is notoriously rich but here, half-fat crème fraîche replaces some of the oil to give a lighter result. The addition of Parmesan cheese and finely chopped anchovy fillets makes for a **really gutsy sauce**.

Don't be put off by the idea of a chicken and fish combination: the anchovy has an affinity with chicken and actually enhances it in an unobvious manner. Mixed with tuna, this also makes a wonderful filling for jacket potatoes.

PER SERVING: 515 calories, 23 g fat

8 Mexican-style soft flour tortillas, 20 cm (8 inches) in diameter
1 cos or romaine lettuce, washed and finely shredded
300 g (10 oz) cooked chicken breasts, sliced
2 hard-boiled eggs, chopped roughly
15 g ($^1/_2$ oz) Parmesan cheese, grated

FOR THE CAESAR DRESSING:
2 tablespoons half-fat crème fraîche
1 teaspoon white wine vinegar
1 teaspoon Dijon mustard
2 tablespoons extra virgin olive oil
2 anchovy fillets, chopped very finely
a pinch of sugar
freshly ground black pepper

1   For the caesar dressing; whisk the crème fraîche, vinegar and mustard together in a bowl. Gradually whisk in the oil. Add the chopped anchovies and season with the sugar and pepper.
2   Lay the tortillas out on a chopping board or work surface. Spoon a couple of teaspoons of dressing over each and, using the back of the spoon, spread the dressing over the entire surface.
3   Scatter the lettuce over the tortillas, followed by the sliced chicken and chopped egg. Sprinkle each with a little grated Parmesan.
4   Fold the bottom quarter of the tortilla up and then fold each side in to enclose the filling. Serve two per person.

MAKES: 4
PREPARATION & COOKING TIME:
20 minutes + marinating overnight + 20 minutes cooking
FREEZING: not recommended

LAMB KEBABS

A traditional Middle Eastern dish, 'shish' kebab is a popular takeaway of **spit-roasted lamb, sliced and served in pitta bread**. If you have time, infuse the lamb with lemon juice, rosemary and garlic overnight, to tenderise and flavour the meat. Serve on a bed of salad and top with either Houmous (page 24) or Tzatziki (page 24).

PER SERVING: 347 calories, 9 g fat

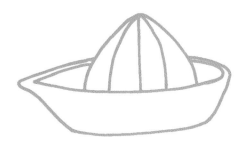

FOR THE MEAT:
450 g (1 lb) lamb neck/shoulder fillet
2 rosemary sprigs, bruised
1 garlic clove, sliced thinly
1 tablespoon olive oil
1 tablespoon lemon juice
freshly ground black pepper

FOR THE SALAD:
1/2 cos or romaine lettuce, washed, dried and shredded
2 ripe tomatoes, cubed
1 small red onion, sliced thinly

TO SERVE:
4 wholemeal or plain pitta breads
Houmous (page 24) or Tzatziki (page 24)

1 Trim any excess fat from the lamb fillets and place in a bowl, with the rosemary and garlic. Pour over the oil and lemon juice. Season with pepper and stir thoroughly to coat the meat. Cover and leave to marinate overnight if possible. Stir a couple of times.

2 Preheat the oven to Gas Mark 9/electric oven 240°C/fan oven 220°C. Place a roasting pan in the oven on the highest shelf.

3 Scrape the rosemary leaves and garlic off the lamb. Place the fillets in the heated roasting pan, taking care as the meat may spit. Cook for 20 minutes. Remove from the oven and allow the lamb to 'rest' for 10 minutes.

4 Lightly toast or warm the pitta breads. Split them horizontally and fill with the salad ingredients. Thinly slice the lamb and divide it between the pockets. Spoon some houmous or tzatziki over the lamb and serve at once.

SERVES: 3
PREPARATION & COOKING TIME:
35 minutes + 20 minutes cooking
FREEZING: not recommended

PER SERVING: 539 calories, 24 g fat

Aside from their takeaway popularity, pizzas seem to have taken over supermarket shelves as well. They are not difficult to make at home and **have the advantage of tasting much fresher**, plus you can calorie-count your toppings. As a compromise you could always buy a ready-made base and do your own topping. Rustica (crushed tomatoes) or passata (sieved tomatoes) are pure tomato, bottled, and make a ready-made, natural sauce. Serve with a mixed leaf salad.

FOR THE BASE:
225 g (8 oz) strong white bread flour
1 teaspoon easy-blend dried yeast
½ teaspoon coarse sea salt
1 tablespoon olive oil

FOR THE TOPPING:
2 teaspoons extra virgin olive oil
150 ml (¼ pint) rustica or passata
1 garlic clove, chopped finely
15 g (½ oz) fresh basil leaves,
a few sprigs reserved for garnish
and the remainder torn
½ x 390 g can of artichoke hearts,
drained and halved
115 g (4 oz) button mushrooms,
wiped and sliced
25 g (1 oz) Italian salami with
peppercorns slices, halved
125 g pack of buffalo mozzarella, drained,
dried and sliced thinly
½ small red onion, sliced thinly
and the rings separated
12 black olives
15 g (½ oz) Parmesan cheese shavings

1 In a mixing bowl, combine the flour, yeast and salt. Make a well in the centre and pour in the oil and 150 ml (¼) pint of warm water. Mix to combine and then tip out on to a work surface and knead for 10 minutes by hand (5 minutes if you have a machine) until the dough is smooth. Place in an oiled polythene bag, in a warm place, for about 15 minutes, while you prepare the pizza topping.

2 Preheat the oven to Gas Mark 7/electric oven 220°C/fan oven 200°C. Grease a baking sheet.

3 Either roll out the dough on a lightly floured work surface or shape with your hands into a 30 cm (12 -inch) round. Place on the greased baking sheet and brush the surface of the dough lightly with 1 teaspoon of the oil, to form a waterproof layer.

4 Smooth the tomato sauce evenly over the surface. Scatter with garlic and basil. Then top with the remaining ingredients, in the order they are listed.

5 Cover loosely with an oiled polythene bag and leave in a warm place for 15 minutes, to enable the dough to puff up slightly.

6 Remove the bag and drizzle the remaining teaspoon of oil over the pizza. Bake in the centre of the oven for 15–20 minutes. Check after 15 minutes and dab off any liquid that has come out of the mushrooms or tomato, with a little kitchen paper. Return to the oven for a further 5 minutes if you like a more crisp pizza.

7 Serve with a sprinkling of Parmesan shavings and basil leaves.

ARTICHOKE, SALAMI & MUSHROOM PIZZA

SERVES: 4
PREPARATION & COOKING TIME:
20 minutes + 30 minutes chilling
+ 55 minutes cooking
FREEZING: not recommended

PER SERVING: 389 calories, 26 g fat

Bought quiches are convenient as a standby to reheat but never quite duplicate the **trembling soft centre that a home-made quiche** has when it comes hot out of the oven. Quiches are often made using cream but I have substituted semi-skimmed milk, to reduce the fat content. Wholemeal pastry raises the fibre content of this dish and the addition of baking powder makes the crust crisper and lighter. Asparagus and Gruyère combine well to make a subtle filling.

ASPARAGUS QUICHE

FOR THE WHOLEMEAL PASTRY:
115 g (4 oz) wholemeal flour
1 teaspoon baking powder
25 g (1 oz) butter or block margarine, diced
25 g (1 oz) white vegetable cooking fat, diced

FOR THE FILLING:
80 g (3 oz) asparagus tips
80 g (3 oz) Gruyère cheese, grated
2 large eggs plus 1 egg yolk
300 ml (10 fl oz) semi-skimmed milk
¹/₂ teaspoon Dijon mustard
freshly ground black pepper

1   For the pastry, mix the flour and baking powder together in a bowl. Rub in the butter or margarine and vegetable fat until the mixture resembles fine breadcrumbs. Sprinkle over 2 tablespoons of cold water and bring it together to form a ball of dough.

2   On a lightly floured surface, roll out the pastry and use it to line a deep 20 cm (8-inch) flan tin. Prick the base with a fork and chill for at least 30 minutes.

3   Preheat the oven to Gas Mark 6/electric oven 200°C/fan oven 180°C. Place a baking sheet on the middle shelf. Put a sheet of foil, greaseproof or baking paper in the flan and fill with baking beans.

4   Bake the pastry case blind for 15 minutes. Remove the foil or paper and beans and return to the oven for a further 5 minutes, until lightly golden.

5   Meanwhile, blanch the asparagus tips in boiling water for 2 minutes. Drain and plunge into cold water to stop cooking.

6   Remove the pastry case from the oven and reduce the temperature to Gas Mark 5/electric oven190°C/fan oven 170°C.

7   Scatter the grated cheese over the base of the pastry case. Whisk together the eggs, egg yolk, milk, mustard and pepper and pour the mixture over the cheese. Drain the asparagus and arrange the tips in a cartwheel shape on top. Return the quiche to the oven and bake for 30–35 minutes, until puffy and golden. Serve warm or cold.

MAKES 6
PREPARATION & COOKING TIME:
25 minutes + 40 minutes cooking
FREEZING: recommended

PER SERVING: 526 calories, 28 g fat

Pasties are a classic example of how just a few, good-quality ingredients can achieve such a delicious result. Best eaten warm, they are also a **natural addition to picnics and lunch boxes**. The turnip and swede are interchangeable, seasoned with just enough herbs to bring out their flavour. Be sure to use steak mince, which has a relatively low fat content (approximately 7 per cent) and will save you the chore of dicing chuck steak into tiny pieces as is the traditional way.

CORNISH PASTIES

FOR THE PASTRY:
350 g (12 oz) plain flour
80 g (3 oz) butter or block margarine
80 g (3 oz) white vegetable fat

FOR THE FILLING:
350 g (12 oz) steak mince
1 potato, weighing about 175 g (6 oz),
peeled, sliced very thinly and
then chopped roughly
1 small turnip, approximately 175 g (6 oz) ,
peeled, sliced very thinly and
then chopped roughly
1 onion, chopped finely
1/4 teaspoon dried mixed herbs
a good pinch of cayenne pepper
milk, for brushing
sea salt and plenty of
freshly ground black pepper

1 Preheat the oven to Gas Mark 7/electric oven 220°C/fan oven 200°C. Lightly grease a baking sheet.
2 For the pastry, rub the butter or margarine and vegetable fat into the flour until the mixture resembles fine breadcrumbs. Sprinkle over 6 tablespoons of cold water and bring it all together to form a ball of dough. Wrap in cling film and chill in the fridge while you make the filling.
3 In a bowl, combine the steak mince, potato, turnip and onion. Add the herbs, and season with salt, pepper and cayenne pepper. Stir in 2 tablespoons of cold water to moisten.
4 Divide the pastry into six. On a lightly floured surface, roll out each piece into a 20 cm (8 -inch) round, making sure that you keep the shape as you roll. Do not

worry if the edges are a little uneven, it just adds to the rugged effect!
5 Dampen the edges with a little of the milk. Place a portion of the meat filling on half of each pastry circle. Fold over the pastry to cover and press the edges together to seal. Then turn the pasties so that the edge points upwards. Press down slightly to give it a flatter base and then crimp the edge with your fingers to form the traditional wavy pattern.
6 Place on the prepared baking sheet. Brush with milk and make two slits near the top of each side, to allow steam to escape. Bake in the middle of the oven for 10 minutes before reducing the heat to Gas Mark 6/electric oven 180°C/fan oven 160°C, for a further 30 minutes, or until the pasties are golden and the filling cooked.

SERVES: 4
PREPARATION & COOKING TIME:
40 minutes
FREEZING: not recommended

PER SERVING: 302 calories, 19 g fat

This is a lovely 'chunky' omelette, **a complete dish cooked in a frying pan**. Ideal as a light lunch, it is equally delicious cold and cuts easily to take on picnics. Vary the ingredients to use those in season. A crisp green salad is all that is needed to accompany.

SPANISH FRITTATA

1 potato, weighing about 225 g (8 oz)
1 tablespoon olive oil
80 g (3 oz) chorizo, sliced thinly and
slices cut into quarters
1 courgette, weighing about 175 g (6 oz),
sliced thinly
1 onion, chopped
6 large eggs, beaten
2 rounded tablespoons
shredded fresh basil leaves
sea salt and freshly ground black pepper

1 Slice the potato very thinly and rinse the slices in cold water to remove excess starch. Dry thoroughly on a tea towel.
2 Heat the oil in a non-stick frying pan, measuring 23 cm (9 inches) in diameter at the base. Arrange the potatoes in a single layer and cook over a medium heat for about 10 minutes, until they are just cooked. Turn frequently.
3 Preheat the grill to high.
4 Add the chorizo, courgette and onion to the pan. Continue to cook for a further 5 minutes, moving the ingredients around the pan every now and then so that they are evenly tinged with brown.

5 Reduce the heat slightly. Whisk a little salt and some pepper into the eggs and pour into the pan. Scatter the basil over the top and cook for 3 minutes, to set the egg underneath.
6 Place the pan under the grill (ensuring that the handle is not directly under the heat) and cook for a further 3–4 minutes, until puffy and golden. Serve hot, at room temperature or cold.

This multi-cultural chapter reflects our seemingly ever-growing love of food from around the world – stir-fries (Sweet & Sour Pork, page 53) and curries (Chicken Korma and Thai Chicken Curry, pages 52 and 44) rub shoulders with the typically British Fish Pie (page 50) and Italian pasta (Spaghetti Carbonara, page 54).

Main meals do take longer to make yourself but the benefits – in terms of taste, nutrition and personal satisfaction – are more than worth it. Making

MAIN MEALS

double and freezing half compensates for the preparation time involved. Takeaways and ready meals are also very expensive if you are feeding a family; and armed with the following recipes as a starting point, I hope you will feel inspired to cook from scratch as often as possible.

SERVES: 4
PREPARATION & COOKING TIME: 25 minutes
FREEZING: not recommended

THAI CHICKEN CURRY

This is a **wonderfully fragrant** dish. The ingredients used are available from large supermarkets. If you can, use galangal in place of ginger, and kaffir lime leaves rather than lime zest, for a truly authentic curry. A reduced-fat coconut milk is now available (containing 45 per cent less fat), and reduced-salt soy sauce makes for a far healthier dish than any ready-made Thai chicken curry. Just be sure to prepare everything in advance, before you commence cooking.

Serve the curry in bowls, on a bed of steamed jasmine rice.

PER SERVING: 335 calories, 14 g fat

- 1 lemon grass stalk
- 1 tablespoon sunflower or vegetable oil
- 450 g (1 lb) skinless, boneless chicken breasts
- 1 red chilli, de-seeded and chopped finely
- 1 teaspoon grated fresh ginger or galangal paste
- 1 garlic clove, crushed
- 225 g (8 oz) chestnut, oyster or shiitake mushrooms, (stalks removed), wiped and halved
- 1 bunch of spring onions, sliced thinly, 1 reserved for garnish
- 300 ml ($^1/_2$ pint) reduced-fat coconut milk
- 150 ml ($^1/_4$ pint) chicken stock
- zest of $^1/_2$ lime, pared in thick strips, white pith removed, or 2 kaffir lime leaves
- 1 rounded tablespoon chopped fresh coriander
- 1 tablespoon reduced-salt soy sauce

1. Remove any tough outer leaves from the lemon grass. Cut the stalk into three and bruise the pieces. Cut the chicken breasts into bite-sized pieces, about eight each.
2. Heat the oil in a wok. Add the lemon grass, chicken, chilli, ginger or galangal and garlic. Stir-fry for 2 minutes, to seal the meat.
3. Stir in the mushrooms and cook for a further minute.
4. Add the spring onions, coconut milk, stock, lime zest or lime leaves, coriander and soy sauce to the wok. Bring to the boil, reduce the heat and simmer gently for 8 minutes or until the chicken pieces are cooked.
5. Remove the lemon grass and the lime zest or leaves. Shred the remaining spring onion and scatter it over to garnish.

SERVES: 4
PREPARATION & COOKING TIME:
30 minutes + 1 hour 20 minutes cooking
FREEZING: not recommended

MOUSSAKA

Moussaka is a little time-consuming to make but does make a **wonderful dish**. Make it ahead and then cook for when your friends arrive, and all it needs is a crisp salad of mixed lettuce leaves and cucumber to accompany. The yogurt-based topping is much quicker than a traditional white sauce and low-fat yogurt can be used instead, for even fewer calories.

PER SERVING: 648 calories, 40 g fat

2 aubergines, weighing about 450 g (1 lb)
450 g (1 lb) cooked waxy potatoes, sliced
2–3 tablespoons olive oil
sea salt
and freshly ground black pepper

FOR THE LAMB SAUCE:
450 g (1 lb) minced lamb
1 large onion, chopped finely
1 tablespoon flour
400 g can of chopped tomatoes
1 fat garlic clove, crushed
2 teaspoons tomato purée
1 tablespoon chopped fresh parsley
1 teaspoon ground cinnamon
1/2 teaspoon dried oregano
1 bay leaf

FOR THE TOPPING:
300 ml (1/2 pint) Greek yogurt
2 eggs, beaten
50 g (2 oz) Parmesan cheese, grated finely
grated nutmeg

1 Remove the stalks and cut the aubergines into 1 cm (1/2 -inch) slices. Layer in a colander, sprinkling a little salt between each layer. Weigh down and leave for 30 minutes to extract any bitter juices.

2 Meanwhile brown the mince and onion in a non-stick pan over a high heat, breaking up any lumps. Reduce the heat and stir in the flour. Cook for 1 minute. Add the chopped tomatoes, garlic, tomato purée, parsley, cinnamon, oregano and bay leaf. Season, bring to the boil, cover the pan, reduce the heat and simmer for 30 minutes, stirring occasionally.

3 Preheat the grill to high. Preheat the oven to Gas Mark 4/electric oven 180°C/fan oven 160°C.

4 Rinse the salt from the aubergines and pat them dry with a tea towel. Arrange in a single layer on the grill pan and brush with half the olive oil. Grill for about 5 minutes, or until golden. Turn, brush with the remaining oil and grill until golden.

5 Lightly grease a 2.3- litre (4- pint) ovenproof dish. Remove the bay leaf from the mince and adjust the seasoning if necessary. Arrange half the aubergine slices over the base of the dish, and half the sliced potato on top of them. Pour the lamb sauce over the top. Finish with the remaining aubergine and potato slices.

6 In a bowl, whisk together the yogurt, eggs and Parmesan. Season and pour over the potato, covering it completely. Sprinkle a little grated nutmeg over the top and bake for about 40 minutes, until puffy and golden.

SERVES: 4
PREPARATION & COOKING TIME:
50 minutes
FREEZING: not recommended

PER SERVING: 597 calories, 21 g fat

1 butternut squash, weighing about 1 kg
(2¹/₄ lb), peeled, seeds removed and cut
into bite-sized pieces
1 tablespoon olive oil
freshly ground black pepper

FOR THE RISOTTO:
50 g (2 oz) butter
1 tablespoon olive oil
350 g (12 oz) risotto rice
1 garlic clove, crushed
1 litre (1³/₄ pints) hot,
good-quality vegetable stock
3 tablespoons sherry
1 teaspoon tomato purée
1 bay leaf
50 g (2 oz) grated Parmesan cheese
115 g (4 oz) rocket
1 tablespoon pine nuts, toasted

Risottos are currently enjoying a well deserved revival
and can stand as a meal on their own. Some crisp pancetta,
scattered on top with the butternut squash, makes a delicious
addition. Alternatively, lightly cooked asparagus tips and smoked
salmon strips with a squeeze of lemon juice make a lovely
summer variation – omit the tomato purée and sherry and
substitute dry white wine for 150 ml (¹/₄ pint) of the stock.

1 Preheat the oven to Gas Mark 7/electric oven 220°C/fan oven 200°C.
2 In a roasting tin, toss the squash with the olive oil and season with freshly ground black pepper. Bake for 30–35 minutes, turning the chunks of squash over halfway through.
3 Meanwhile, heat 25 g (1 oz) of the butter with the olive oil in a non-stick frying pan. Stir in the rice and garlic and cook for 2–3 minutes, until the rice is transparent.
4 Gradually add a little of the hot stock, plus the sherry, tomato purée and bay leaf. Allow the rice to absorb the liquid before pouring in some more stock, a ladleful at a time.
5 Simmer, uncovered, for 15–20 minutes, until the rice is tender and most of the stock has been used. Stir occasionally.
6 Remove the bay leaf. Stir in the remaining butter, most of the grated Parmesan and the rocket. Season.
7 Spoon the risotto on to serving plates. Scatter the roasted butternut squash on top and sprinkle with toasted pine nuts and the remaining Parmesan.

ROASTED BUTTERNUT SQUASH & ROCKET RISOTTO

SERVES: 6
PREPARATION & COOKING TIME:
50 minutes + 45 minutes cooking
+ 15 minutes standing
FREEZING: recommended

PER SERVING: 346 calories, 15 g fat

9 sheets no-need-to-pre-cook lasagne verde
freshly ground black pepper

FOR THE TOMATO SAUCE:
2 x 185 g cans of tuna in sunflower oil
1 small onion, chopped finely
1 garlic clove, crushed
400 g can of chopped tomatoes
115 g (4 oz) baby button mushrooms,
wiped and halved
2 teaspoons tomato purée
a pinch of sugar
2 rounded tablespoons snipped fresh basil
1 tablespoon drained capers

FOR THE CHEESE SAUCE:
40 g (1½ oz) butter or margarine
40 g (1½ oz) plain flour
425 ml (¾ pint) semi-skimmed milk,
warmed
50 g (2 oz) mature Cheddar cheese, grated
25 g (1 oz) Parmesan cheese, grated finely
½ teaspoon Dijon mustard

Try this version and I **guarantee that you won't be disappointed**. What is more, it is ideal for those trying to cut down on their red meat intake (the mushrooms themselves have that meat-like 'bite' element about them!) and, likewise, the tuna sauce makes an excellent partner for pasta. Serve with a salad of crisp mixed green leaves, cucumber, red pepper and slices of avocado.

1   Preheat the oven to Gas Mark 5/electric oven190°C/fan oven 170°C. Grease a 1.75-litre (3-pint) shallow, square dish.
2   Drain the tuna, reserving 2 teaspoons of the oil. Break up the fish slightly.
3   Heat the reserved oil in a saucepan and cook the onion and garlic for 5 minutes, without browning, until softened. Add the tomatoes, mushrooms, tomato purée and sugar and season with pepper. Bring to the boil, reduce the heat, cover, and simmer for 10 minutes. Stir in the flaked tuna, basil and capers. Adjust the seasoning.
4   Meanwhile, make the cheese sauce. Melt the butter, stir in the flour and cook for 1 minute. Gradually blend in the milk, bring to the boil and simmer for a couple of minutes. Stir in two-thirds of the Cheddar and Parmesan and season to taste with mustard and pepper.
5   Spoon a couple of tablespoons of cheese sauce over the base of the serving dish. Then arrange three sheets of lasagne over the top. Spoon half the tuna sauce over these and pour over a third of the remaining cheese sauce. Repeat the pasta, tuna and cheese sauce layers. Finish with the remaining lasagne. Pour the rest of the cheese sauce over the top, making sure that you cover the dried pasta, and sprinkle with the reserved cheeses.
6   Bake in the centre of the oven for 40–45 minutes, until golden. Allow the lasagne to stand for 15 minutes before serving. This allows any liquid to be fully absorbed.

TUNA, TOMATO & MUSHROOM LASAGNE

SERVES: 4
PREPARATION & COOKING TIME:
1 hour + 30 minutes cooking
FREEZING: recommended

PER SERVING: 543 calories, 28 g fat

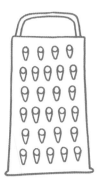

FOR THE LAMB:
450 g (1 lb) minced lamb
1 large onion, chopped
1 tablespoon flour
150 ml (¼ pint) good lamb stock
115 g (4 oz) button mushrooms,
wiped and sliced finely
2 tablespoons chopped fresh parsley
1 bay leaf
freshly ground black pepper

FOR THE CHEESY POTATO AND
LEEK TOPPING:
700 g (1½ lb) potatoes,
peeled and quartered
25 g (1 oz) butter or margarine
2 leeks, sliced very finely
3 tablespoons semi-skimmed milk
80 g (3 oz) Cheddar cheese, grated

Traditionally, shepherd's pie is made from lamb and cottage pie with beef. The easiest version is made using leftovers from roast lamb, mixed with gravy and topped with creamed potato. As there are six of us in our family, such leftovers never materialise, so I have started from scratch. Adding 'hidden' vegetables is an easy way of boosting your intake of them – **mushrooms with the lamb and sautéd leeks stirred into the mashed potato**.

1 Brown the mince and onion in a non-stick pan over a high heat, breaking up any lumps. Reduce the heat and stir in the flour. Cook through for 1 minute. Gradually blend in the stock. Add the mushrooms, parsley and bay leaf and season to taste with pepper. Bring to the boil, cover the pan and then reduce the heat and simmer for 30 minutes, until the lamb is cooked. Stir occasionally.

2 Preheat the oven to Gas Mark 6/electric oven 200°C/fan oven 180°C. Grease a 2- litre (3½- pint) ovenproof dish.

3 Place the potatoes in a pan with cold water, bring to the boil, cover and simmer for 15–20 minutes, or until cooked.

4 Meanwhile, melt the butter or margarine and sauté the leeks over a low heat for 10 minutes until softened, but not brown.

5 Drain the potatoes and return to the heat to dry off any excess moisture. Mash until lump free. Beat in the leeks, milk and 50 g (2 oz) of the cheese. Adjust the seasoning to taste.

6 Remove the bay leaf from the mince and pour into the prepared dish. Spoon the potato over the top and roughly smooth the surface. Sprinkle with the remaining grated cheese and bake for 30 minutes, until the top is crisp and golden. Alternatively brown under a hot grill, whichever is more convenient.

COOK'S NOTE: If making in advance and cooking the pie straight from the fridge, it will take about 45 minutes to heat through thoroughly.

SHEPHERD'S PIE

SERVES: 4
PREPARATION & COOKING TIME:
40 minutes + 45 minutes cooking
FREEZING: not recommended

PER SERVING: 503 calories, 19 g fat

Cod or haddock both work well with this recipe. Serve traditionally, with peas.

Including some cooked spinach in the base could make a dinner party variation of this pie. Use a mixture of white wine and stock instead of milk for the sauce and slices of cooked potato for the topping.

FISH PIE

FOR THE POTATO TOPPING:
675 g (1¹/₂ lb) potatoes, peeled and quartered
3 tablespoons semi-skimmed milk
25 g (1 oz) butter or margarine
sea salt and freshly ground black pepper

FOR THE PARSLEY SAUCE:
40 g (1¹/₂ oz) butter or margarine
40 g (1¹/₂ oz) plain flour
425 ml (³/₄ pint) semi-skimmed milk, warmed
a squeeze of lemon juice
1 tablespoon chopped fresh parsley
freshly ground black pepper

FOR THE FILLING:
450 g (1 lb) white fish fillets, skinned and cut into 2.5 cm (1-inch) cubes
115 g (4 oz) cooked prawns
2 hard-boiled eggs, quartered

1 Preheat the oven to Gas Mark 6/electric oven 200°C/fan oven 180°C. Place a baking sheet on a high shelf. Butter a 2 - litre (3¹/₂-pint) shallow ovenproof dish.
2 Place the potatoes in a large pan with cold water, bring to the boil, cover, and simmer for about 15–20 minutes, or until cooked.
3 Meanwhile, make the parsley sauce. Melt the butter, stir in the flour and cook for 1 minute. Gradually blend in the milk, bring to the boil and simmer for a couple of minutes. Stir in the lemon juice and chopped parsley and season to taste with freshly ground black pepper.

4 Arrange the white fish cubes, in a single layer, over the base of the prepared dish. Scatter on the prawns and place the hard-boiled eggs on top. Pour over the parsley sauce, covering the fish completely.
5 Drain the potatoes and return to the heat to dry off any excess moisture. Mash the potatoes until lump free. Beat in the milk and butter and season to taste. Spoon equally over the fish and sauce. Smooth the top and then fork through a pattern. Bake for 45 minutes, until the fish is cooked and the potato golden.

SERVES: 4
PREPARATION & COOKING TIME:
50 minutes + 20 minutes cooking
FREEZING: not recommended

CHICKEN KORMA

If you have never tried making a curry before, then this is where to start! **An easy-to-follow recipe**, using spices that you will probably have to hand anyway (or at least have heard of!). The yogurt base makes it a low calorie, yet creamy, sauce. This is more of a spicy than a 'hot' dish.

Accompany with a pilau of jasmine or basmati rice (see Cook's tip.)

PER SERVING: 512 calories, 34 g fat

4 tablespoons sunflower or vegetable oil
3 onions
3 garlic cloves, crushed
2 teaspoons grated fresh root ginger
1 tablespoon ground coriander
1½ teaspoons ground cumin
1 cinnamon stick, halved
½ teaspoon ground turmeric
10 green cardamom pods, seeds removed and ground
4 cloves, ground or a pinch of ground cloves
2 bay leaves
4 skinless, boneless chicken breasts, weighing about 450 g (1 lb) in total, cut into 8 chunks each
50 g (2 oz) flaked almonds
425 ml (¾ pint) Greek yogurt
2 teaspoons cornflour
a squeeze of lemon juice
sea salt and freshly ground black pepper
fresh coriander leaves, to garnish

1 Heat 2 tablespoons of oil in a non-stick wok or large frying pan. Thinly slice one of the onions and fry for about 10 minutes, until crisp and brown. Drain on kitchen paper. Keep warm.
2 Heat the remaining oil. Finely chop the remaining onions. Fry, with the garlic and ginger, for about 10 minutes, until soft and golden.
3 Reduce the heat. Add the spices and bay leaves and cook for a couple of minutes.
4 Stir in the chicken pieces and almonds. Blend in 150 ml (¼ pint) of cold water. Combine the yogurt and cornflour (this helps to prevent the sauce from curdling) and gradually stir into the chicken mixture. Season to taste with salt and pepper. Bring to a simmer, cover, and cook for 15–20 minutes, stirring occasionally.
5 Remove the cinnamon sticks and bay leaves. Squeeze in a little lemon juice and adjust the seasoning to taste. Serve on a bed of pilau rice, topped with the browned onion rings, and scattered with coriander leaves.

COOK'S TIP To make pilau rice for the perfect accompaniment, first rinse 225 g (8 oz) of jasmine or basmati rice well. Sauté in a little oil with some chopped onion before cooking it in 350 ml (12 fl oz) boiling stock, with ½ teaspoon turmeric, a handful of sultanas, a few cardamom pods, a cinnamon stick and a bay leaf.

SERVES: 4
PREPARATION & COOKING TIME: 25 minutes
FREEZING: not recommended

SWEET & SOUR PORK

From a faint memory, I think that this was probably the first Chinese dish that we Westerners decided we could possibly attempt to reproduce. What a change now – the supermarket shelves are flooded with a reflection of our love for, not only Chinese cuisine but Indian, Italian, Thai and numerous other influences!

Making your own sweet and sour is straightforward, and infinitely preferable to glutinous jars of 'sludgy' bought sauce. Traditionally, the pork is fried in a batter coating – here is a simplified, one-pan version, in which the meat is stir-fried, thus also cutting back on the calories. Substitute chicken for the pork, if you prefer.

PER SERVING: 307 calories, 10 g fat

FOR THE SAUCE:
3 tablespoons cider vinegar
3 tablespoons soft brown sugar
2 tablespoons reduced-salt soy sauce
1½ tablespoons tomato purée
150 ml (¼ pint) pineapple juice

FOR THE STIR-FRY:
2 tablespoons sunflower oil
350 g (12 oz) pork fillet/tenderloin, sliced into 1 cm (½-inch) medallions, then halved
1 onion, chopped roughly
½ red pepper, de-seeded and cut into 2 cm (¾-inch) pieces
½ green pepper, de-seeded and cut into 2 cm (¾-inch) pieces
225 g can of bamboo shoots, drained and rinsed
1½ tablespoons cornflour, blended with 2 tablespoons water

1 Combine the vinegar, sugar, soy sauce and tomato purée in a small bowl. Make the pineapple juice up to 225 ml (8 fl oz) with water and stir into the sauce.
2 Heat 1 tablespoon of the oil in a wok or large frying pan. Add the pork and stir-fry over a high heat, turning the meat continuously, for 1–2 minutes, until browned. Remove from the pan and set aside.
3 Add the remaining oil to the pan. Stir-fry the onion and peppers for 1 minute. Return the pork to the pan and add the sauce and bamboo shoots. Bring to the boil, reduce the heat, cover and simmer for 5 minutes.
4 Remove the lid, stir in the cornflour mixture and bubble until the mixture thickens. Heat through, stirring all the time, for 1 minute. Serve at once, on a bed of rice or egg noodles.

SERVES: 4
PREPARATION & COOKING TIME:
10 minutes + 10 minutes cooking
FREEZING: not recommended

PER SERVING: 524 calories, 17 g fat

This is a dream to make; you can **rustle it up in next to no time!** It also has the added bonus of being lower in calories than its shop-bought, glutinous counterparts, as it uses fromage frais rather than cream. The only point to watch is not to return the pan to the hob after you have added the sauce – otherwise the eggs will scramble; just allow the heat of the pasta to cook it through.

SPAGHETTI CARBONARA

350 g (12 oz) spaghetti
1 tablespoon olive oil
175 g (6 oz) dry-cured back bacon, snipped into pieces
3 eggs, lightly beaten
4 tablespoons grated Parmesan cheese
4 tablespoons fromage frais
freshly ground black pepper

1 Bring a large pan of salted water to the boil, add the spaghetti and cook as directed on the packet.
2 Heat the oil in a frying pan. Add the bacon and fry over a high heat for about 5 minutes, until crisp and golden.
3 Beat together the eggs, Parmesan and fromage frais. Season with pepper to taste.

4 Drain the pasta well and return it to the saucepan, away from direct heat. Discard all but 1 tablespoon of fat from the bacon, and add this plus the bacon, making sure that you scrape in those tasty, crunchy bits that get stuck to the bottom of the pan as well.
5 Pour in the egg mixture and mix everything together. Keep stirring until the spaghetti is thoroughly coated and the sauce is creamy and smooth. Serve at once, with some steamed seasonal green vegetables.

The ideas for this chapter lie at the heart of what this book is all about, because the right choices made in childhood can formulate our eating patterns for life. We establish our personal preferences, and a concept of what it is right to eat, when we are still children and both of these will affect our long-term good health.

Peer-pressure and the power of advertising certainly have as great an influence on children as that of Mum and Dad. Most parents realise that

WHIZZ KIDS

their children like at least some kinds of fast food. I have taken the staples from children's menus (Crispy Chicken Dippers, page 58, Home-made Quarter Pounders, page 61 and Fish in Breadcrumbs, page 57) and converted them into far healthier, tastier options to make at home. Fast food is, after all, only popular food converted into mass-produced form. Here I am simply reversing the process, and giving you the confidence to provide the type of food which children like, with the added bonus that it is actually good for them.

SERVES: 4
PREPARATION & COOKING TIME: 35 minutes
FREEZING: recommended, for sausage sauce only

PER SERVING: 585 calories, 23 g fat

FASTA PASTA

Canned tomatoes provide an **instant sauce** for this tasty family sausage and pasta dish. If making just for adults, add a little red chilli when cooking the sausages to spice them up a bit. Use butcher's best sausages, which have a higher meat content and are lower in fat than cheaper versions, plus a guaranteed superior taste!

2 teaspoons olive oil
1 onion, chopped
450 g (1 lb) good-quality sausages
1 garlic clove, crushed
1 tablespoon red wine vinegar
400 g can of chopped plum tomatoes in tomato juice or 425 ml
  ($^3/_4$ pint) rustica (crushed tomatoes) or passata (sieved tomatoes)
2 heaped tablespoons chopped fresh parsley, plus extra to garnish
2 teaspoons tomato purée
$^1/_2$ teaspoon dried oregano
$^1/_2$ teaspoon brown sugar
1 bay leaf
300 g (10 oz) pasta, e. g. spirals or penne
freshly ground black pepper

1 Heat the oil in a non-stick frying pan. Add the onion and cook for a couple of minutes, until beginning to soften.
2 Meanwhile, remove the skin from the sausages and break into bite-sized pieces. Add to the pan, with the garlic, and cook over a medium heat for 4–5 minutes, to brown.
3 Stir in the red wine vinegar and bubble for 1 minute. Add all the remaining sauce ingredients and simmer, uncovered, for 10 minutes while you cook the pasta. Stir occasionally, to prevent sticking.
4 Cook the pasta according to the manufacturer's instructions.
5 Remove the bay leaf from the sauce. Drain the pasta and stir it into the sauce. Adjust the seasoning, if necessary, pile on to serving plates, garnish with chopped parsley and serve at once.

SERVES: 4
PREPARATION & COOKING TIME: 15 minutes
FREEZING: not recommended

PER SERVING: 259 calories, 7 g fat

TUNA MINI MUFFIN PIZZAS

Children love pizza but all too often the bought varieties are heavily laced with E-numbers, additives, salt and unidentifiable flavours. These **bread muffins are speedy to make** and the basic principle can be used for endless combinations – encouraging the children to choose their own toppings means that they are far more likely to eat their food up! French bread, or thick slices from a large, day-old loaf, also make a good base for pizza. Canned sweetcorn kernels with peppers are a useful standby in place of fresh.

4 bread muffins
about 3 tablespoons rustica (crushed tomatoes)
  or passata (sieved tomatoes)
a good pinch of dried mixed herbs (optional)
185 g can of tuna in sunflower oil, drained and flaked
4 tablespoons cooked sweetcorn kernels
$^1/_4$ red pepper, de-seeded and chopped finely
50 g (2 oz) mozzarella cheese, grated
4 teaspoons grated Parmesan cheese

1 Preheat the grill to medium-high. Halve the muffins horizontally and toast for about 1 minute on each side.
2 Spread the cut side of each muffin with 1 teaspoon of rustica or passata. Sprinkle on a few herbs, if using, and then the tuna, sweetcorn and pepper. Finish off with grated mozzarella and parmesan.
3 Replace the muffins under the grill and cook for 1–2 minutes, until the cheese is bubbling and golden. Serve at once.

SERVES: 4
PREPARATION & COOKING TIME: 10 minutes + 20 minutes cooking
FREEZING: not recommended

PER SERVING: 180 calories, 3 g fat

FISH IN BREADCRUMBS

The value of fish in the diet depends mainly on how it is cooked. Steamed fish is relatively low in fat, but deep-frying it in a batter coating catapults it to the opposite end of the healthy-eating spectrum! Replacing the batter with breadcrumbs, and baking rather than frying, significantly reduces the calorie count whilst at the same time **enabling the flavour of the fish to shine through**. This is a wonderful way of cooking fish for all the family. Serve with Wedgies (page 58) and home-made Tomato Ketchup (page 30). Halibut, cod and plaice all work well for this recipe.

450 g (1 lb) white fish fillets, skinned and boned
25 g (1 oz) plain flour, seasoned
1 large egg, beaten
50 g (2 oz) fairly stale, very fine breadcrumbs
spray oil (see Cook's note) or 1½ tablespoons olive oil

1 Preheat the oven to Gas Mark 8/electric oven 230°C/fan oven 210°C. Line a lipped baking sheet with foil and position towards the top of the oven.
2 Rinse the fish and pat dry.
3 Take three plates. Place the flour on one, egg on another and the breadcrumbs on the last.
4 Dip one fillet at a time into the flour, to coat it evenly, and shake off any extra. Then dip in the egg. Hold it up to allow any excess to run off. Finally coat each side with breadcrumbs. Repeat with the remaining fish.
5 Spray the foil on the baking tray with oil. Arrange the fish in a single layer and spray the top of each lightly with oil. Alternatively, drizzle with a little olive oil.
6 Bake for 15–20 minutes (depending on the thickness of the fish) until the flesh is just cooked and the coating is crisp and golden.

COOK'S NOTE: Spray oil is ideal for this recipe – a fine mist lightly coats the fish, using far fewer calories and resulting in a more even finish, than drizzling oil over.

SERVES: 4 as an accompaniment
PREPARATION & COOKING TIME: 15 minutes + 20 minutes cooking
FREEZING: not recommended

PER SERVING: 136 calories, 4 g fat

BEANS WITH A KICK!

A fabulously spiced-up version of baked beans, these go really well with Cornish Pasties (page 41) to 'pep' you up on a cold winter's day. Conversely, they would be a great dish to serve cold with barbecued meats in the summer. Using canned beans cuts out the need for the rather laborious and time-consuming soaking and pre-cooking needed when using the dried variety. If you prefer, replace the traditional haricots with their close relatives, cannellini beans.

1 tablespoon olive oil
1 onion, chopped finely
1 garlic clove, crushed
420 g can of haricot beans, drained and rinsed
150 ml (¼ pint) passata (sieved tomatoes)
1 tablespoon tomato purée
1 tablespoon Worcestershire sauce
1 tablespoon black treacle
½ teaspoon mustard powder
½ teaspoon soft brown sugar
freshly ground black pepper

1 Heat the oil in a medium-sized saucepan. Add the chopped onion and garlic and cook for about 5 minutes, without browning, to soften.
2 Stir in all the remaining ingredients, plus 150 ml (¼ pint) of water. Bring to the boil, reduce the heat and simmer, uncovered, for 20 minutes, until the sauce is slightly reduced, thick and shiny. Adjust the seasoning and serve hot or cold.

SERVES: 6
PREPARATION & COOKING TIME:
15 minutes + 20 minutes cooking
FREEZING: recommended

SERVES: 4
PREPARATION & COOKING TIME:
5 minutes + 30 minutes cooking
FREEZING: not recommended

CRISPY CHICKEN DIPPERS

These dippers are unrecognisable from the bought variety, which are invariably coated in a thick batter or crumbs and deep-fried, resulting in a high fat content. The **crumb coating on these dippers is a thin, crisp layer** – you can see the breast meat through it in places. They are straightforward to make and you can adapt the seasoning at will – for example, add 1 teaspoon of dried oregano to the crumbs for a change. Delicious served hot or cold – and adults will find these equally moreish. Tomato Salsa (page 26) makes a good accompaniment.

PER SERVING: 237 calories, 10 g fat

115 g (4 oz) fine white breadcrumbs
40 g (1¹/₂ oz) finely grated Parmesan cheese
450 g (1 lb) boneless, skinless chicken breasts
1 large egg
1 tablespoon milk
2 tablespoons olive oil
sea salt and freshly ground black pepper

1 Mix together the breadcrumbs and Parmesan on a dinner plate.
2 Thinly slice the chicken breasts into strips, about 7 cm (3 inches) long by 2.5 cm (1 inch) wide. You should make about ten from each breast.
3 Beat together the egg and milk. Season with salt and pepper.
4 Preheat the grill to medium-high.
5 Dip strips of chicken in the egg mixture and then coat with the breadcrumbs. Shake to remove any excess and arrange in a single layer on the grill pan. You will need to cook these in two batches.
6 Drizzle with a little oil and grill for 4–5 minutes on each side, until the coating is crisp and golden and the chicken is cooked through.

WEDGIES

These **chunky potato chips** are tossed in a little olive oil and baked rather than fried; they have the extra advantage of keeping their skins on, so retaining the nutrients immediately underneath, and they have more fibre than chips. Roasted Garlic & Chive Dip (page 26) goes well with these.

PER SERVING: 165 calories, 4 g fat

700 g (1¹/₂ lb) potatoes (Maris Piper or King Edwards are good)
1 tablespoon olive oil
sea salt and freshly ground black pepper

1 Preheat the oven to Gas Mark 8/electric oven 230°C/fan oven 210°C.
2 Scrub the potatoes, halve them lengthways, cut each half into three lengths and rinse in cold water to get rid of excess starch. Pat dry with a clean tea towel.
3 Place the potatoes in a bowl and toss in the oil. Spread out on a baking tray and season.
4 Bake on a high shelf for 30 minutes, turning halfway through, until crisp and golden.

COOK'S NOTE: For a spiced-up version, toss the wedgies in the oil and then a mix of 2 teaspoons ground cumin, 1 teaspoon paprika, 1 teaspoon dried oregano, ¹/₄ teaspoon mild chilli powder and ¹/₈ teaspoon sea salt. Stir in a crushed garlic clove and bake.

MAKES 16
PREPARATION & COOKING TIME:
20 minutes + 45 minutes resting
+ 20 minutes cooking
FREEZING: not recommended

PER ROLL: 98 calories, 4 g fat

These little bundles, **wrapped up cosily in their own snuggle sacks**, fuse the border between pastry-cased sausage rolls, and 'all-in one' hot dogs! They are best eaten, either hot or cold, on the day of making, and make an excellent addition to picnics or packed lunches, with a little pot of home-made Tomato Ketchup (page 30) to accompany. Bread has a far lower fat content than the traditional pastry. Make sure that the sausages are good quality, with a high meat content, and so comparatively low in fat.

225 g (8 oz) Cumberland sausages
I small egg, beaten

FOR THE DOUGH:
225 g (8 oz) strong white bread flour
I teaspoon easy-blend yeast
$^{1}/_{2}$ teaspoon coarse sea salt
I tablespoon olive oil

1 Make the dough first. In a mixing bowl, combine the flour, yeast and salt. Make a well in the centre and pour in the oil and 150 ml ($^{1}/_{4}$ pint) of warm water. Mix to combine and then tip out on to a work surface and knead for 10 minutes by hand (5 minutes if you have a machine) until the dough is smooth. Place in an oiled polythene bag in a warm place for 15 minutes, to allow the dough to 'relax' enough for it to be rolled out.
2 Grease a baking sheet with a lip.
3 Roll out the dough into an oblong measuring 30 x 24 cm (12 x 9$^{1}/_{2}$ inches). Cut in half to make two 30 cm (12 -inch) long strips.
4 Remove the skins from the sausages. Form the sausagemeat into two, equal-sized, balls. Using wetted hands, form each ball into a 30 cm (12 -inch) length, keeping the diameter as even as possible.
5 Brush the surface of each strip of dough with beaten egg. Place the sausage strips at the edge of each length, and roll up firmly, to form a very long sausage. Make sure that the edges are sealed.
6 Cut into 4 cm (1$^{1}/_{2}$-inch) lengths. Arrange on the baking sheet, allowing room for them to expand a little, and brush with egg. Cover with oiled cling film, and leave in a warm place for about 30 minutes, until they have puffed up a little. (Do not leave the sausagemeat for too long in a warm atmosphere.)
7 Preheat the oven to Gas Mark 7/electric oven 220°C/fan oven 200°C.
8 Remove the cling film and brush the rolls with egg wash again. Bake in the centre of the oven for 15–20 minutes, until the cases are golden and the sausage in the centre is cooked.

COOK'S NOTE: Try spreading a little grainy mustard over the sausages, or sprinkle grated Cheddar on top of the dough.

SAUSAGE ROLLS

MAKES: 4
PREPARATION & COOKING TIME:
10 minutes + 30 minutes chilling (optional)
+ 14 minutes cooking
FREEZING: recommended

PER SERVING: 195 calories, 6 g fat

Beefburgers were probably the food that inspired the theme for this book. They have had extensive bad press coverage over the past few years but, love them or hate them, the undisputed fact remains that many children (and adults) relish eating them. It is not all bad news though – red meat is a valuable source of iron, zinc and B-vitamins, and modern breeding methods have led to leaner meat being produced. In fact, burgers are **easy to make from scratch at home**, with the added bonus that you can be sure what has gone into them. Use a mince with about a 15 per cent fat content – you do need some fat to achieve the best texture – too little and the resulting burger tends to be dry. I have added onion, herbs and horseradish sauce for flavour, removing the need for any added salt.

450 g (1 lb) lean beef mince
25 g (1 oz) fresh breadcrumbs
1 small onion, grated or chopped very finely
1 teaspoon dried mixed herbs
1 teaspoon creamed horseradish sauce
(optional)
1 small egg, beaten
freshly ground black pepper

1 Preheat the grill to high.
2 Place the mince, breadcrumbs, onion, herbs, horseradish and pepper in a large bowl. Mix well to combine thoroughly.
3 Add enough egg to bind the mixture together.
4 Using wetted hands, divide the meat into four and shape into round patties, approximately 10 cm (4 inches) in diameter and 2.5 cm (1 inch) thick. If you have time, place on a plate, cover, and refrigerate for at least 30 minutes, to allow the beefburgers to firm slightly.
5 Cook under the preheated grill for 5–7 minutes on each side, until browned and cooked through. Serve hot with Tomato Salsa (page 26) and Wedgies (page 58) and a green salad.

HOME-MADE QUARTER POUNDERS

MAKES: 2 batons, 6 servings
PREPARATION & COOKING TIME:
10 minutes + 15 minutes cooking
FREEZING: recommended, uncooked

PER BATON: 263 calories, 12 g fat

Garlic bread is **a favourite with all ages**. It is quick and easy to make, and you can suit your taste by adding more herbs (chives, tarragon and thyme are all good); or why not sprinkle some grated mozzarella in between the bread slices? Reduced-fat butter spread cuts down on the calories considerably and its consistency makes it easy to blend in the other ingredients.

GARLIC BREAD

115 g (4 oz) reduced-fat butter spread
2 garlic cloves, crushed
1 tablespoon chopped fresh parsley
a good squeeze of lemon juice
2 x 35 cm (14 -inch) French bread batons
freshly ground black pepper

1 Preheat the oven to Gas Mark 6/electric oven 200°C/fan oven 180°C. Place a baking tray in the centre of the oven.
2 Beat together the spread, garlic, parsley, lemon juice and black pepper.
3 Slice the batons, almost all the way through but just leaving a hinge, at 4 cm (1½-inch) intervals. (This is wider than usual, so you'll need to use less butter, thus cutting down on calories!)
4 Spread the butter between the slices, smearing any remaining over the top of the loaves. Wrap loosely in foil.
5 Bake for 10 minutes. Fold back the foil and return to oven for a further 4–5 minutes to crispen. Serve at once.

Puddings need not be fattening but they are often perceived as having indulgent overtones because the sweet course is an 'extra', not really needed to satisfy hunger. However, sensible eating need not totally rule out any foods or type of recipe if we seek alternatives to high-fat or sugar ingredients or perhaps just eat less of these!

Virtually all of the recipes in this chapter are fruit based and hence

DESSERTS

make a valuable contribution to the diet in the form of vitamins and fibre. For those which require dairy products (such as Light Lemon Cheesecake, page 70) I have used low-fat alternatives.

The basic ideas behind many of the following recipes can be adapted to use your own favourite ingredients, for example you can vary the fruits in Almond Plum Crumble (page 68) and Bramley Apple Pie (page 67) to create desserts that are right for you.

SERVES: 8
PREPARATION TIME: 20 minutes + 4–5 hours freezing
FREEZING: essential!

PER SERVING: 473 calories, 33 g fat

SERVES: 6
PREPARATION & COOKING TIME: 20 minutes + chilling
FREEZING: recommended – but not in a glass dish!

PER SERVING: 388 calories, 24 g fat

ORANGE, GINGER, CHOCOLATE & PRALINE ICE CREAM

TIRAMISÙ

A whole range of ice creams are now on the market, from those that contain plenty of additives and no cream at all to glorious conglomerations of pure decadence. Below I have offered a halfway house, a combination based half on yogurt and half on cream.

FOR THE PRALINE:
80 g (3 oz) pecan nuts or flaked almonds
80 g (3 oz) granulated sugar

FOR THE ICE CREAM:
450 g tub of Greek yogurt
284 g jar of orange and ginger high-fruit-content spread
50 g (2 oz) luxury dark chocolate, chopped into small chunks
300 ml (¹/₂ pint) double cream

1 Preheat the oven to Gas Mark 4/electric oven 180°C/fan oven 160°C. Lightly oil a baking tray.
2 Toast the nuts in the oven for 6–8 minutes, until browned. Transfer to the oiled baking tray.
3 Heat the sugar in a heavy-based saucepan over a low to medium heat, until it melts. Watch it carefully all the time and shake the pan occasionally to make sure that the sugar dissolves evenly. Once it starts to brown, remove from the heat and swirl around the pan until it turns golden. (It will continue to cook in the pan.) Pour over the nuts and leave to cool. Once cold, blitz in a blender to a coarse powder.
4 In a bowl, beat together the yogurt, fruit spread, chocolate pieces and praline.
5 Freeze in a shallow container for about 2 hours or until the mixture is just starting to set around the edge.
6 Lightly whip the cream until it just holds its shape. Whisk the semi-frozen mixture until smooth and then carefully beat in the cream. Return to the freezer and leave until firm. Leave at room temperature for 10 minutes before serving.

This classic Italian dessert seems to be the black forest gâteau of the 2000s! Tiramisù is to be found on many restaurant menus and in the chilled cabinet of most supermarkets. The good news is that it is very easy to make, and **actually tastes better the next day**, so is an ideal choice if you are entertaining.

I have exercised some 'damage limitation' on the calorie front, by substituting fromage frais for the traditionally used raw eggs. This pudding also looks stunning in individual glasses.

24 sponge fingers
125 ml (4 fl oz) strong espresso coffee, cooled
4 tablespoons marsala or sweet sherry
5 tablespoons icing sugar
250 g tub of mascarpone
200 g tub of fromage frais
50 g (2 oz) plain chocolate, minimum-70% -cocoa -solids, grated cocoa powder or icing sugar, to decorate (optional)

1 Arrange half of the sponge fingers in the base of a 20 cm (8 -inch) round glass dish.
2 Combine the coffee, 2 tablespoons of marsala or sherry and 1 tablespoon of icing sugar, and drizzle half of this, evenly, over the sponge fingers.
3 In a small bowl, beat together the mascarpone, fromage frais, remaining marsala or sherry and icing sugar, until smooth.
4 Spread half the mixture over the soaked sponges and scatter half the grated chocolate over the top.
5 Dip the remaining sponge fingers in the coffee mixture, and arrange on top. (Do this with about three fingers at a time.) Repeat the mascarpone and chocolate layers.
6 Chill for at least 2–3 hours before serving. Serve dusted with either a little sifted cocoa powder or icing sugar if you like.

SERVES: 4
PREPARATION & COOKING TIME:
5 minutes + 8 minutes cooking
FREEZING: not recommended

Yogurt, essentially a healthy product, now swamps the dairy produce section in various guises, usually over sweetened and flavoured with synthetic pseudo-fruit purées. Here is a very simple, yet healthy version.

2 tablespoons sunflower seeds
2 tablespoons hazelnuts, chopped roughly
2 teaspoons sesame seeds
1 rounded tablespoon raisins
225 g (8 oz) ripe strawberries, sliced roughly
500 g tub of low-fat natural 'bio' yogurt

HOME-STYLE
STRAWBERRY YOGURT

PER SERVING: 216 calories, 12 g fat

1 Preheat the oven to Gas Mark 6/electric oven 200°C/fan oven 180°C.
2 Spoon the sunflower seeds, hazelnuts and sesame seeds into a shallow baking tray. Toast in the oven for about 8 minutes, until golden brown. Do keep a careful eye on them though, as they burn quickly. Remove from the oven and cool. Stir in the raisins.
3 Divide the sliced strawberries between four glass tumblers. Spoon the yogurt equally over the top of each. Sprinkle with crunchy nutty seed topping and serve at once.

SERVES: 6
PREPARATION TIME: 15 minutes
FREEZING: not recommended

Somehow, the small effort that goes into making a fruit salad transforms an everyday fruit bowl into something special, with minimum effort. Make just prior to serving so as to maximise the nutrients (vitamin C starts to be lost as soon as fruit and vegetables are cut).

3 kiwi fruit
2 ripe mangoes
2 passion-fruit
2 large bananas
juice of 1 lime
1½ tablespoons ginger and lemongrass cordial
2 pieces of stem ginger

MANGO, BANANA
& KIWI FRUIT SALAD

PER SERVING: 117 calories, 0 g fat

1 Peel the kiwi fruit, halve and slice. Place in a serving bowl.
2 To prepare the mangoes, slice down each side of the long stone and remove the skin from the three resulting pieces. Cut the flesh into irregular chunks, removing as much of the flesh from the stone as possible, and add to the bowl.
3 Halve the passion-fruit and scoop the seeds and juice into the bowl.
4 Peel and slice the bananas and add to the fruit salad. Stir in the lime juice and cordial.
5 Rinse and pat the stem ginger dry. Slice into very thin matchsticks and sprinkle over the salad before serving.

SERVES: 2
PREPARATION TIME: less than 5 minutes!
FREEZING: not recommended

The 21st century's version of milkshake, smoothies are packed with vitamins and bursting with natural flavour. Below is a basic guideline for you to devise your own creations from – based on banana as the thickening agent. For a breakfast variation, omit the apple juice and use 2 tablespoons of natural organic 'bio' yogurt, made up to 150 ml (¼ pint) with semi-skimmed milk.

1 ripe Comice pear
1 ripe banana
50 g (2 oz) fresh raspberries
150 ml (¼ pint) pure, unsweetened apple juice, chilled

RASPBERRY
& PEAR SMOOTHIE

PER SERVING: 123 calories, 0 g fat

1 Peel and quarter the pear. Roughly chop and place in a blender.
2 Peel the banana. Break into four pieces and add to the blender, with the raspberries and apple juice.
3 Liquidise until smooth and divide between two glasses. Serve at once.

SERVES: 4–6
PREPARATION & COOKING TIME:
25 minutes + 30 minutes chilling
+ 40 minutes cooking
FREEZING: recommended

PER SERVING: 305 calories, 13 g fat

A well known gentleman makes 'exceedingly good' apple pies, and an equally well known fast-food chain sells their deep-fried version. Here is the healthy option – although you won't be able to take it away (as it has no pastry on the bottom, thus saving on the calories).

A fruit pie is **such a traditional English dish, using the simplest ingredients**, and it can include any fruits that are plentiful – plums, apricots, rhubarb and gooseberries, to name but a few. This recipe contains 900 g (2 lb) of fruit, which makes a big dome under the pastry crust to begin with but subsides during cooking.

BRAMLEY APPLE PIE

FOR THE PASTRY:
**40 g (1¹/₂ oz) butter or
block margarine, cubed
40 g (1¹/₂ oz) white vegetable fat, cubed
175 g (6 oz) plain flour**

FOR THE FILLING:
**50 g (2 oz) caster sugar plus about
1 teaspoon for sprinkling
1 rounded tablespoon cornflour
900 g (2 lb) Bramley cooking apples, peeled,
cored and sliced thinly
1 tablespoon elderflower cordial (optional)
milk, for brushing**

1 For the pastry, rub the butter and vegetable fat into the flour until the mixture resembles fine breadcrumbs. Sprinkle over 2 tablespoons of cold water and bring it all together to form a ball of dough. Knead very gently until just smooth. Wrap in cling film and chill for 30 minutes.

2 Preheat the oven to Gas Mark 5/electric oven 190°C/fan oven 170°C.

3 For the filling, mix together sugar and cornflour. In an 850 ml (1¹/₂-pint) pie dish, layer the sliced apples with the sugar and cornflour mixture, packing the fruit down well. Pour the elderflower cordial, if using, over the top.

4 On a lightly floured surface, roll out the pastry to 2.5 cm (1 inch) larger than the top of the pie dish. Cut off a 2.5 cm (1-inch) strip all around the outside of the pastry. Brush the rim of the pie dish with milk, then lightly press the strip of pastry on to it. Brush the pastry strip with some more milk and lift the remaining pastry on to it, to make a lid. Pinch the edges to seal and make a decorative pattern with thumb and forefingers, or a fork.

5 Brush the top with milk and sprinkle with a little caster sugar. Using a sharp knife, make a cross in the centre to allow steam to escape. Place on a baking sheet and cook on a high shelf in the oven, for about 40 minutes, until the pastry is golden, and the apples soft. Serve hot with custard (make this while the pastry is chilling), or cold.

SERVES: 4–6
PREPARATION & COOKING TIME:
15 minutes + 45 minutes cooking
FREEZING: recommended

PER SERVING: 309 calories, 14 g fat

There is something about cooked plums – I think it lies in the consistency of the liquid which their natural juices make when combined with sugar – that results in such a fabulous base for crumbles. I have purposely been generous in the ratio of fruit to crumble topping, to reduce the fat and sugar content while upping the proportion of fruit.

Rhubarb, with some powdered ginger rubbed into the crumble topping, would make a delicious alternative. Crumble just wouldn't be the same without its traditional companion, custard. To help reduce the calories, make it with skimmed or semi-skimmed milk.

675 g (1½ lb) plums, washed, halved and stoned
50 g (2 oz) golden granulated sugar

FOR THE CRUMBLE:
115 g (4 oz) plain flour
50 g (2 oz) golden granulated sugar
50 g (2 oz) butter
50 g (2 oz) ground almonds
25 g (1 oz) flaked almonds

1 Preheat the oven to Gas Mark 4/electric oven 180°C/fan oven 160°C. Grease a 1.75 -litre (3 -pint) shallow ovenproof dish.
2 Arrange the plums in a single layer in the prepared dish. Sprinkle enough sugar to sweeten over the top.
3 Place the flour and sugar in a bowl. Rub in the butter until the mixture resembles fine breadcrumbs. Stir in the ground almonds and half the flaked almonds.
4 Scatter the crumble mixture over the plums and press down lightly. Sprinkle the reserved flaked almonds over the top.
5 Bake in the centre of the oven for 40–45 minutes, until the crumble is golden and the plums are cooked. Serve hot or warm.

ALMOND PLUM CRUMBLE

SERVES: 10
PREPARATION TIME: 30 minutes + chilling
FREEZING: recommended

PER SERVING: 314 calories, 21 g fat

Cheesecakes are notoriously fattening and so unlikely to feature in a healthy eating book. However, on the basis of **'a little of what you fancy does you good'**, I have included this one, using low-fat dairy products, which we are lucky enough to now have the option of buying readily from supermarkets. Ginger biscuits would make a nice variation in place of digestives in the base.

LIGHT LEMON CHEESECAKE

FOR THE BASE:
50 g (2 oz) butter or block margarine
4 oz (115 g) digestive biscuits, crushed

FOR THE TOPPING:
I sachet of powdered gelatine
juice and grated zest of 2 lemons
200 g tub of light cream cheese
250 g tub of ricotta cheese
200 ml tub of half-fat crème fraîche
115 g (4 oz) caster sugar
150 ml ('/₄ pint) double cream
I rounded tablespoon home-made
or good-quality lemon curd

1 Lightly grease a 20 cm (8 -inch) spring-clip cake tin and base-line the tin with greaseproof paper.

2 To make the base, melt the butter. Stir in the crushed digestive biscuits. Using the back of a spoon, press them evenly over the base of the prepared tin. Chill in the fridge while you make the topping.

3 In a small bowl, sprinkle the gelatine over the juice of I lemon. Stand over a pan of hot (not boiling) water and stir until dissolved. Remove from the heat and leave to cool a little.

4 Using a wooden spoon, mix together cream cheese, ricotta, crème fraîche, caster sugar and lemon zest until smooth. Slowly beat in the remaining lemon juice.

5 Gradually whisk in the gelatine in a thin stream, stirring all the time.

6 Lightly whisk the cream until slightly thickened but still of a pouring consistency. Carefully fold into the cheese mixture and pour over the biscuit base. Gently shake the tin to level the surface.

7 Spoon the lemon curd in a rough spiral over the top of the cheesecake. Using a skewer, swirl through randomly to give a decorative effect. Chill until set, about 3–4 hours.

8 When ready to serve, loosen gently around the edge and open out the tin. Slide a palette knife between the biscuit base and greaseproof paper and ease the cheesecake on to a serving plate.

This chapter sets out to show how you can indeed 'have your cake and eat it'!

While I am in no way suggesting that cakes should form a major part of your diet, there is nothing wrong with eating them in moderation. Food is for pleasure as well as for nourishing us, and I hope that in this chapter I have drawn the

CAKES & BARS

two concepts closer together. Many of the recipes contain fruit, itself a natural sweetener. All are obviously free from the additives that bought cakes contain – colourings to enhance their appearance, preservatives to prolong shelf life and artificial flavourings attempting to make them comparable to home-baking.

MAKES: approximately 24
PREPARATION & COOKING TIME: 15 minutes + 14 minutes cooking
FREEZING: recommended

PER COOKIE: 50 calories, 2.5 g fat

WHITE-CHOCOLATE-CHIP & APRICOT COOKIES

Few can resist a chocolate-chip cookie and these never last long! Here is a lower-fat version, using reduced-fat butter spread. These are **deliciously crisp, crumbly and chewy at the same time!** Try using raisins and sunflower seeds for a change, or substitute the apricots and white chocolate with shelled peanuts and milk or plain chocolate.

115 g (4 oz) low-fat butter spread
115 g (4 oz) golden caster sugar
¹/₂ teaspoon vanilla extract
1 large egg yolk
150 g (5 oz) plain flour
115 g (4 oz) white chocolate, chopped roughly into fairly small chunks
50 g (2 oz) no-need-to-soak dried apricots, chopped finely

1 Preheat the oven to Gas Mark 4/electric oven 180°C/fan oven 160°C. Lightly grease two baking sheets or line them with baking parchment.
2 Cream together the low-fat butter spread, sugar and vanilla extract, until light and fluffy.
3 Beat in the egg yolk.
4 Fold in the flour, followed by the chopped chocolate and dried apricots. Mix well.
5 Place heaped teaspoonfuls of the mixture on greased baking sheets, spacing well apart, to allow room to spread. Flatten slightly with a wetted fork.
6 Bake in the centre of the oven for 12–14 minutes, until golden. Transfer at once to a rack and leave to cool.

PREPARATION & COOKING TIME: 20 minutes + 1 hour cooking
FREEZING: recommended

PER SLICE: 286 calories, 14 g fat

BANANA PECAN TEABREAD

Cakes made using the rubbing-in method generally have the advantage of being much lower in fat and sugar than creamed cake mixtures.

We often eat this teabread as a pudding – warm from the oven. Be sure to use ripe bananas, as these have the best flavour. As a variation, omit the nuts and stir in some dried fruit, such as chopped dates or sultanas, with the sugar.

275 g (10 oz) self-raising flour
1 teaspoon bicarbonate of soda
1¹/₂ teaspoons ground cinnamon
115 g (4 oz) butter or margarine
115 g (4 oz) light muscovado sugar
450 g (1 lb) ripe bananas (about 3 medium bananas), mashed
2 large eggs, beaten
2 tablespoons milk
80 g (3 oz) pecan nuts
warmed, sieved apricot jam, or clear honey, to glaze

1 Preheat the oven to Gas Mark 4/electric oven 180°C/fan oven 160°C. Grease and line a 900 g (2 lb) loaf tin. (I find foil easiest for this.)
2 Sift the flour, bicarbonate of soda and cinnamon into a bowl.
3 Rub in the butter or margarine, until the mixture resembles fine breadcrumbs. Stir in the sugar.
4 Add the bananas, eggs and milk. Stir to combine and pour into the prepared tin. Smooth to level the surface. Scatter the pecans evenly over the top.
5 Bake in the centre of oven for about 1 hour (depending on the shape of your tin) or until a skewer inserted in the middle, comes out clean. Check the top after about 45 minutes. If it is browning too much (the nuts are susceptible to burning), cover with a piece of foil.
6 Remove cake from oven and cool on a wire rack. Brush with the jam or honey glaze, to give a shiny finish, and serve warm or cold.

MAKES: 15 squares
PREPARATION & COOKING TIME:
20 minutes + 45 minutes cooking
FREEZING: recommended

AMERICAN CARROT CAKE

This is popular at many sandwich and coffee bars and is always a welcome ingredient in lunchboxes – for big and little people! Typically sickly sweet (Americans do tend to go totally overboard in the cake and pudding departments!), I have cut down on the fat and sugar content, resulting in an 'Anglo' version. This is a **lovely fragrant cake** – the carrot being enhanced with **mellow spices** – that is delicious warm from the oven. Alternatively, leave it to cool and finish with the cream - cheese icing, if you're not counting the calories!

PER SQUARE: 336 calories, 22 g fat

225 g (8 oz) self-raising flour
1½ teaspoons baking powder
1 tablespoon ground mixed spice
1 teaspoon ground ginger
175 g (6 oz) golden caster sugar
50 g (2 oz) walnut halves, chopped roughly
3 large eggs, beaten
200 ml (7 fl oz) sunflower oil
½ teaspoon vanilla extract
225 g (8 oz) finely grated carrot

FOR THE ICING:
175 g (6 oz) low-fat cream cheese
25 g (1 oz) butter or margarine, softened
80 g (3 oz) icing sugar, sifted
lemon juice
vanilla extract
15 walnut halves, to decorate

1 Preheat the oven to Gas Mark 4/electric oven 180°C/fan oven 160°C. Grease and base-line a shallow tin, 17 x 26 cm (6½ x 10½ inches).

2 In a large bowl, sift together the flour, baking powder and spices. Stir in the sugar and walnuts.

3 Make a well in the centre and add the eggs, oil and vanilla extract. Stir until smooth. Mix in the carrot and spoon into the prepared tin. Level the surface and bake in the centre of the oven for 40–45 minutes, until a metal skewer inserted in the middle comes out clean. Allow to cool in tin for 10 minutes before turning out on to a wire rack to cool.

4 To make the icing, beat together the cream cheese and butter or margarine in a bowl, until smooth. Gradually add the sifted icing sugar, followed by a squeeze of lemon juice and a few drops of vanilla extract, to taste.

5 Spread the icing evenly over the cake's surface. Mark into 15 squares and decorate each with a walnut half. Cover with cling film, to prevent it from drying out, and keep refrigerated.

MAKES: 15
PREPARATION & COOKING TIME: 20 minutes + 30 minutes cooking
FREEZING: recommended

PER BROWNIE: 175 calories, 15 g fat

BOSTON BROWNIES

The Americans lead the world in the realms of fast food and this is another scrumptious example of their influence, found in most take-away sandwich bars over here now. Free from E-numbers and additives, these **moist**, (almost verging on stodgy!) squares are **packed with nuts** – almonds, walnuts and brazils also go well, or for children, substitute chocolate drops instead.

115 g (4 oz) plain chocolate, minimum 70% cocoa solids,
    broken into pieces
115 g (4 oz) butter or margarine
2 large eggs, beaten
1 teaspoon vanilla extract
100 g (3½ oz) macadamia nuts, chopped
50 g (2 oz) plain flour
½ teaspoon baking powder

1 Preheat the oven to Gas Mark 4/electric oven 180°C/fan oven 160°C. Grease and line a shallow baking tin measuring 28 × 18 cm (11 × 7 inches).
2 Melt the chocolate and butter or margarine in a bowl set over a pan of hot water. Remove from the heat, stir until smooth and then leave to cool slightly.
3 Whisk in the beaten eggs and vanilla extract.
4 Stir in three-quarters of the nuts. Sift together the flour and baking powder and fold in.
5 Pour into the prepared tin and shake to level the surface. Sprinkle the reserved nuts evenly over the top and place on the middle shelf of the oven. Bake for 25–30 minutes, until the middle is just firm (it does continue to cook slightly when taken out of the oven) and the mixture has started to come away from the edges of the tin.
6 Cool in tin for 10 minutes before cutting into 15 squares and transferring to a wire rack to cool completely.

MAKES 15
PREPARATION & COOKING TIME: 15 minutes + 30 minutes cooking
FREEZING: not recommended

PER SERVING: 137 calories, 7 g fat

APRICOT OATJACKS BARS

These chewy bars, with **almost more filling than outside**, make a delicious alternative to the bought varieties – ideal for lunchboxes or as a snack. The apricots, wholemeal flour and oats mean that they have the added advantage of being high in fibre, and dried apricots are also an excellent source of iron and vitamin A. I often use dates in place of the apricots.

175 g (6 oz) no-need-to-soak dried apricots, snipped into small pieces
juice of 1 orange
80 g (3 oz) self-raising wholemeal flour
80 g (3 oz) rolled porridge oats
80 g (3 oz) light muscovado sugar
1 teaspoon ground mixed spice
115 g (4 oz) butter or block margarine
1 tablespoon golden syrup

1 Preheat the oven to Gas Mark 4/electric oven 180°C/fan oven 160°C. Lightly grease a square baking tin measuring 18 × 18 cm (7 × 7 inches).
2 Place the apricots and orange juice in a small pan and simmer uncovered, for about 10 minutes, until the orange juice is absorbed and the apricots have softened. Leave to cool.
3 Combine the flour, oats, sugar and spice in a mixing bowl.
4 Gently melt together the butter or margarine and syrup. Cool before pouring on to the dry ingredients. Stir well to combine.
5 Put just over half the mixture in the tin and smooth evenly over the base. Spoon the apricot purée over the top, using a knife to spread. Dot pieces of remaining oat mixture over the surface – there will be a few gaps, but that is fine as it enables you to see some of the apricot.
6 Bake on the middle shelf of the oven for 25–30 minutes until golden. Carefully mark into 15 bars. Leave in the tin to cool completely, which prevents the bars from crumbling when they are removed.

MAKES: 12 'man-sized' muffins
PREPARATION & COOKING TIME:
20 minutes + 30 minutes cooking
FREEZING: recommended

PER MUFFIN: 183 calories, 7 g fat

These are **the real McCoy, larger than life, American style!** Muffins are good for packed lunches and also make a great pudding, served warm, with custard. They are very easy to make as they only require mixing, so why not let the children have a go – they are the next generation of cooks, after all – and what an achievement to see that they can make even better-tasting muffins than the supermarket!

80 g (3 oz) butter or margarine
225 g (8 oz) plain flour
2 teaspoons baking powder
1/2 teaspoon bicarbonate of soda
115 g (4 oz) golden granulated sugar, plus 2 teaspoons for sprinkling
225 ml (8 fl oz) natural 'bio' yogurt
1 large egg, beaten
1/2 teaspoon vanilla extract
175 g (6 oz) blueberries, washed and dried

1   Preheat the oven to Gas Mark 4/electric oven 180°C/fan oven 160°C. Set out 12 paper muffin cases on a baking sheet, or use to line large bun tins if you have them.
2   Melt the butter or margarine and allow to cool slightly.
3   Sift the flour, baking powder and bicarbonate of soda into a large bowl.
4   Stir in the sugar. Make a well in the centre of the dry ingredients and add the butter, yogurt, beaten egg and vanilla extract. Stir to just combine. The mixture will look lumpy – this is fine – over mixing will make the muffins heavy and tough.
5   Carefully fold in the blueberries, taking care not to break them up. Divide between muffin cases and sprinkle a little sugar over the top of each.
6   Bake in the centre of the oven for about 30 minutes, until the muffins are risen and crisp on the top. Cool on a wire rack or eat warm.

BLUEBERRY MUFFINS

rice:
  extra-special fried rice 33
  roasted butternut squash and rocket
    risotto 46
  risotto, roasted butternut squash and
    rocket 46
roasted garlic and chive dip 26

salads:
  cranberry, blue cheese, pear and walnut
    salad 18
  Mexican bean salad 21
  Moroccan couscous salad 22
  warm chilli beef salad 20
salsa, tomato 26
sauces:
  barbecue sauce 28
  bolognese sauce 29
  marie-rose sauce 25
  mild curry sauce 25
  tomato ketchup 30
  tomato salsa 26
sausage rolls 60
shepherd's pie 49
shopping 10
smoothie, raspberry and pear 66
soups:
  'cream' of mushroom soup 17
  hot tomato soup 16
  minestrone soup 14
spaghetti carbonara 54
spanish frittata 42
strawberry yogurt, home-style 66
sunflower and sultana coleslaw 16
sweet and sour pork 53

teabread, banana pecan 72
Thai chicken curry 44
tiramisù 64
tomato ketchup 30
tomato salsa 26
tomato soup, hot 16
tortillas, peppered steak, with charred
  vegetables 34

tuna mini muffin pizzas 56
tuna, tomato and mushroom lasagne 48
tzatziki 24

warm chilli beef salad 20
wedgies 58
white chocolate-chip and apricot cookies 72
wrap, chicken caesar 36

yogurt, home-style strawberry 66